Dishes *with* Dashers

Dishes *with* Dashers

ENTERTAINING WITH PANACHE

KATIE DASHWOOD

Quiller

First published in the UK in 2008
by Quiller, an imprint of Quiller Publishing Ltd

British Library Cataloguing-in-Publication Data
A catalogue record for this book
is available from the British Library

ISBN 978 1 84689 037 6

Illustrations by Megan Hess
Designed and typeset by Paul Saunders
Printed in China

Quiller
An imprint of Quiller Publishing Ltd

Wykey House, Wykey, Shrewsbury, SY4 1JA
Tel: 01939 261616 Fax: 01939 261606
E-mail: info@quillerbooks.com
Website: www.countrybooksdirect.com

For RAA 1944–2000. Beloved friend, wonderful dining and travelling companion. A great host, he entertained with his own blend of charismatic wit and style which still sparkles.

Contents

Acknowledgements 8
Introduction 11

The Art of the Party 17

Soups, Starters and Salads 25

Kitchen Suppers in Kitten Heels 71
Fish 72
Poultry 84
Game 92
Meat 102

Puddings 113

Sauces, Standbys and Sides 137

Picnics, Déjeuner sur l'herbe *and Dining Alfresco* 169

The Larder and the Cook's Equipment 183

Index 189

Acknowledgements

My thanks are due to Rosie de Courcy who introduced me to Heather Holden-Brown, my friendly agent who, in turn, opened the appropriate doors for me at Quiller Publishing.

Also to John Beaton, Andrew and Gilly Johnston, Rob Dixon and the rest of the team at Quiller for their unstinting enthusiasm, encouragement and support.

To Gail Dixon-Smith, whose patient red ink corrections and attention to detail made sense of my (at times) rather too casual manuscript!

To Megan Hess – her imaginative illustrations capture the essence of the book so distinctively.

To Paul Saunders – talented designer.

To Richenda Deutsch – my self-styled scullery maid and right hand helper at Dishes with Dashers courses as well as the creator of the catchphrase 'Tips from the Sink' box. A breath of sheer fresh air, she epitomises the word 'generous'.

To all those friends and acquaintances – old and new alike – who attend my Dishes with Dashers courses. If they have derived even half as much fun from these as I have then I will know I am doing something right!

A Recipe for Today, Tomorrow and Everyday

This poem was taken – with permission – from Laura Greenall's collection of recipes. I wrote it out in my best homespun calligraphy hand and RA pinned it on the Notice Board in the kitchen at Cornwell Hill Farm. It has moved with me ever since the house was sold.

Take a heaped cup of Patience
And a big helping of Love
Add two handfuls of Generosity
To all of the Above

Blend in a dash of Laughter
And some Understanding too
Sprinkle generously with Kindness
Add Memories of old and new

Add a lot of Faith and mix well
To make it rich and sweet
Enjoy a heaping portion
With everyone you meet

Introduction

FOR ME, THERE ARE DEFINITELY different foods for different moods – each one evocative of a particular time, place and occasion. It's all a question of enjoying the right thing at the right moment. Be it fish and chips in newspaper, a bacon sarni with melted butter dripping down the chin; a wild sea-bass – gunmetal grey – parcelled up with fennel and herbs, and slung on the barbecue on a starry night; gooey chocolate cake; seared foie gras; Heinz tomato soup or *la grande bouffe* in some rock 'n' roll restaurant – each one has its own moment of glory and is loved for its unique virtues.

Unlike most cooks, I came to the kitchen relatively late in life. The most notable culinary achievement of my childhood was unquestionably the mudcake, splendidly heaped into a paper cupcase, that I triumphantly offered a friend of my parents. At that age and stage, horses, dogs and an assortment of other four-legged animals combined with the attractions of an outdoor existence proved considerably more alluring than any desire to wield a wooden spoon or whisk up soufflés. Leaving aside a quick lick of the cake mixture bowl I spent very little time anywhere near the stove. That is not to say, however, that I did not garner an appreciation of good, honest food. We had our own chickens and sheep as well as a burgeoning vegetable garden, and my father shot and fished so I grew up understanding the importance of quality ingredients even if, in winter months, I would admonish him about the excessive number of pheasants brought to the table! We were, however, united in our worship of oysters – there could never be enough, let alone too many – though we were both firmly of the opinion we had to return to our native Ireland to find the very best.

My culinary baptism of fire began when, aged twenty-one, I went to work and live in London. Here, necessity won the day. My modest salary was never going to enable me to afford to entertain if I intended buying convenience foods. It became obvious, therefore, that I would have to roll up my sleeves and teach myself to cook. I still cringe, though, when I look back at those early attempts to produce food for friends. Over-elaborate, over-fussy dishes – nouvelle cuisine was at its zenith then and pretty patterns on plates dominated – would eventually appear after hours of fraught labour and an evening spent slaving at the stove rather than in the company of my guests. And the awful truth is, the results could not possibly have ever hoped to tantalise the tastebuds. I mean, by the time you have hollowed out courgettes and stuffed them with carrots, what chance can there possibly be of identifying any real flavours?

Fashions in foods change, however, and as I became increasingly captivated by cooking so I began to discover that it is the freshest ingredients which make the best food. My initial belief that only recipes of a complex nature would pass muster gave way to acceptance that the better one's ingredients, the less one had to do to them – other than let their true flavours speak for themselves. When all is said and done, good cooking is all about having the courage to leave well alone or, as Tamasin Day-Lewis puts it so succinctly, '…about having the confidence to subtract rather than add ingredients, about bringing out the essence of the thing itself…'

At around this time, I was lucky enough to meet two great chefs who both inspired and further enhanced my interest in cuisine. The first, Christian Germain – chef/patron of Chateau de Montreuil – has probably been the most single seminal influence on my love of food and cooking, and I spent many happy hours in his kitchen at Montreuil. Christian cooks from the heart and, like all true Frenchmen, with love, passion and spontaneity. Our days would begin with an early morning raid on the fish markets of Boulogne. Forget your traditional *petit déjeuner* – when we returned to the kitchens and watched Christian work his magic on our haul – the standard croissants and coffee were replaced with oysters and scallops straight from the shell and perhaps even a glass of St Veran! He instilled in me a whole host of different cooking methods, the basics of good sourcing as well as saucing and the importance of balancing the textures and flavours of a menu. The notes I made on those visits – a happy, chaotic juxtaposition of metric and imperial measurements punctuated throughout with an eclectic mix of culinary franglais – have become my own epicurean bible, the bedrock of my knowledge and I still refer back to them constantly. True, the standards of a Michelin starred kitchen are at huge variance with the more limited parameters of a domestic one so it is to Christian's credit that his repertoire can withstand being successfully translated to these more modest surroundings.

To Shaun Hill I also owe a huge debt of gratitude. In those days he was based at

Gidleigh Park and his Devonian HQ provided me with many invaluable tips as I observed him and his team produce exquisite dishes for his customers. I gleaned from him how a chef judged the reactions of his clients, not so much from the expression on their faces but more explicitly – how the plates looked when they came back to the kitchen. They told him everything about the way in which the dish had been received. The generosity of these two artistes revolutionised my ideas about food and how to handle it with confidence, and their patience in allowing me to ask endless questions has been the foundation for so much fun and enjoyment derived from cooking and eating – not least of all this book.

Eight years ago I set up my demonstration style sessions – Dishes with Dashers – upon which this book is based. The emphasis of these courses is on using fresh, seasonal produce that is transformed into quick, slick dishes with their own little twist of sophistication. This trademark defines cooking in my kitchen for my way of life. I am a relaxed cook – and seldom bother to weigh or measure out ingredients so a little more or less of a certain item is not going to mar the end result of a dish. I always urge people to taste, taste and taste again when cooking and to adjust seasonings accordingly. I am a self-confessed fiend when it comes to salt and have no time for those who say they only cook without it. I am quite sure their virtuousness is right and proper in terms of health but I fail to see how anyone can expect food to taste of anything without it – and in fairly generous handfuls. But perhaps my determination to use it stems from a boy-friend who claimed he couldn't eat any foods which contained seasoning and nor did he ever waste an opportunity to remind everyone of this woeful tale. This was especially embarrassing in restaurants when the head waiter would be summoned and told all about his 'allergy' and the chef instructed likewise. Curiously though, during the time of our friendship each little dish (seasoned as usual) I set down in front of him, sanctimoniously and sweetly assuring him it was devoid of any such devilish additives, was happily con-sumed. I rest my case!

Whatever you may choose to do with these recipes is entirely up to you as they are not designed to be set in stone but more to be a springboard for your own ideas and interpretation. Or, as the French say, you have a blank canvas so go away and paint it! Oven temperatures are approximately accurate rather than totally exact as anyone who owns an Aga will understand only too well. As a largely self-taught cook, I have often learned the hard way and I hope my various tips and hints will help you avoid some of the errors I have made. Believe me, I have plummeted the depths of culinary ignorance at times!

For me, cooking is about confidence, common sense and time management, and the methods employed herein are the ones which I find work best for me. We all lead busy lives and, more often than not, need to rustle up something quick and delicious whilst multi-tasking. For this reason, I am not a great advocate of the deep-freeze as I find the delights of frozen foods often remove that element of impulse so essential to the instinctive cook.

Cooking is not a means to an end, nor should it be looked upon as a point scoring exercise when it is really an entrée to so much else. I like to look upon it as a unifying factor which brings people together to savour and enjoy all it offers. I cook for pure pleasure and I hope this book will encourage you to do likewise. Certainly, the whole joy of cooking should be for each of us to put an individual stamp on a dish through our own special brand of passion and instinct. Whichever and whatever, the thrills and pleasures of food are never ending – its evolution is forever forward. Hence, there is still so much to learn, to experiment with, to test, to try out and, naturally, to taste, taste and taste. At the end of the day, the fact that all cooking is there to share is one of the things I love best about food. And I use the word 'share' with force and vigour. For me, good cooks are united by their generosity of spirit. For them, it is a delight and a privilege to divulge their recipes to others and to pass on their own special tips and secrets. Mean cooks, on the other hand, are not a recognised breed when it comes to gourmet and gourmand circles.

To encapsulate, I believe good cooking is about the following four 'Ss':

Savvy sourcing and shopping. Seek out the finest and wherever possible, organic foods. Don't be afraid to smell, touch, feel and even ask for a sample taster. Furthermore, if a specific ingredient you require is not available then ask for it to be ordered for you. Think of it from a shopkeeper's point of view – how encouraging for them to have customers who actually care and take a keen interest in what it is they buy and who are not afraid to experiment with something new.

Supporting local suppliers and not supermarkets. Butchers, fish and cheesemongers, farmers and their own weekly markets, farm shops as well as individual artisans, plus the enterprising organic box schemes, who put so much in to their specialised craft, all deserve our custom and loyalty.

Seasonality. Nothing can rival the unfolding of each new season's bounty – asparagus, lamb and sea trout in spring; summer's soft berries and baby broad beans amongst a host of goodies from the garden; oysters, mushrooms and game in the autumn to knobbly root vegetables, chestnuts and cranberries in the depths of winter. To bring these and so many other treats to the table in their prime peak, after a frisson of anticipation, is to enjoy food at is best – as nature intended.

Simplicity. Follow the 'less is best' rule and let the flavours of the finest ingredients speak for themselves.

Bon appétit!

Notes

- All recipes serve 4 – unless otherwise stated.

- Measurements and quantities are given in both Metric and Imperial. It is best to work throughout a recipe using one or the other and not to mix the two.

- A glass (of something) usually refers to around 110 ml (4 fl oz).

- Chicken stock, unless otherwise specified, is home-made (see page 138). Tubs of fresh stock from the supermarket may be substituted though it will not achieve the same jellied consistency as your own.

- Seasoning refers to freshly ground sea salt, Maldon is my first choice, and either whole black or white peppercorns, also freshly ground from a mill. For paler coloured foods, I tend to use the latter simply because with these, cosmetically speaking, black specks look rather unattractive but this is purely a matter of personal preference.

- Butter is unsalted.

- Sugars are unrefined, whenever possible.

- Herbs are fresh, unless otherwise stated.

- Olive oil(s). I tend to use a lightish one for cooking, having several intermediate standard makes on the go at once, and keep the very best Extra Virgin varieties in their smart dark green designer bottles for drizzling over salad leaves.

- Eggs are always fresh, free-range and, unless otherwise stated, large sized.

- Crème fraîche is always the full-fat variety. Half fat does not work in sauces.

- Meat comes from my butcher and is, therefore, always British. Always be guided by your butcher who will know what is best, the provenance of what he is selling and for how long each particular piece has been hung. Furthermore, he will cut and trim it to your own requirements. If boned out, the meat should always come with a bag containing the bones – good for the stockpot!

- Similarly, my fish comes from the fishmonger. Once again, his job is not only for the purpose of selling his produce but also to advise his customers on what is best on the day and to then prepare what it is you have selected. Believe me, his deft knife skills when boning and skinning a fish will save the more ham-fisted of us hours at home!

The Art of the Party

The art of dining well is no slight art, the pleasure not a slight pleasure

MICHEL DE MONTAIGUE 1533–92

I AM OFTEN ASKED WHAT IS the real recipe for a successful party. For me, the quintessential ingredient is the people. What greater compliment than to be hailed as the guest who lights up a room on arrival and thereafter 'sings for their supper'? For them, piles of invitations are routine stuff, whereas the killjoys like Norman-No-Mates will remain home alone. The accomplished host, too, will have mastered the art of ensuring his party always goes with a swing. First, he has the confidence and knack of putting together a heady cocktail of different types of people and age groups to create a dynamic mix. Second, the canny host implements a carefully considered seating plan which produces original discussion and sparkling conversation. The quick-witted host is always mindful of that wonderful catchphrase, 'If you owe a bore dinner – then send it to him'. Once this criterion is in place, apart from the food itself, thoughtful organisation, common sense and time management are the only requirements.

That is not to say, however, that at some stage in our lives, we haven't all been terrorised by the thought of entertaining, especially solo. Certainly, as a newly single hostess, the mere idea of opening the door for even the most casual, low-key little soirée initially invoked waves of panic and had me reaching for the nerve-steadying Kalms pill bottle. I wondered how anyone ever arranged a party without stress but with dash and panache. True, the threat of fused ovens, bolshy Agas, dogs who make off with the joint, curdled sauces, invitees with an awesomely long list of allergies, to mention nothing of an impromptu chimney fire(!) will always overwhelm if one allows such minor hindrances to rule the roost. But the important thing to remember is that a relaxed and happy host imbues in their friends and guests the very same bonhomie. It's an enviable talent to make people feel cosseted and special and, for them, nothing is more flattering.

So, whilst parties should major on hospitality the food, of course, does have a role to play – the tactics for which should never really change. The real art lies in its selection and, wherever appropriate, a little culinary trickery. Often, in an attempt to be lavish and show off, the menu is too rich and far too complicated and means the cook/host spends the entire evening with the pots and pans rather than with their legs under the table. Forget fancy frippery, what is wrong with potted shrimps and shepherd's pie? Absolutely nothing and usually there is a great deal right with this homely duo. Bacchanalian feasts belong in a past era when there were armies of staff to do the fetching and carrying, cooking and waiting at table. Nowadays it's a do-it-yourself show for most of us so it's best to concentrate on planning courses which hang together, are well balanced, and easy to eat and digest. In essence, food should not dominate the proceedings and nor should the occasion become an intense scrutiny of precisely how each ingredient has been marinated, braised, seared, stewed, etc. etc. What a yawn! This isn't about highfaluting cheffy trends – just remember, there are always Michelin-starred restaurants for that ultimate dining experience. If it makes life simpler, resist the temptation to feel obliged to produce the routine trilogy and aim instead for what is most practical. Post-theatre – for example – it is perfectly acceptable for a plate of salami and some olives to replace a starter and even to skip it entirely, or for fruit and cheese to take the place of pudding. When all is said and done, no one really 'needs' three courses – it's only that we have come to 'expect' them and, frequently, everyone welcomes the opportunity to escape the onslaught of a marathon dining experience. Be prepared also, especially when offering shellfish, to have an alternative little something to hand. It is not necessarily always to everyone's liking.

Bear in mind the workload involved when deciding what to cook and eat, reserving one's energies to produce one exceptional dish and cocooning and surrounding it with straightforward adjuncts. Ideally, aim for foods that can be prepared in advance wherever possible and, for the main course, something that can be swiftly transferred from oven to serving dishes, with the minimum delay involved for carving etc. One labour-saving device I always employ is what I call my 'One Stop Dishes', i.e. all the components – meat or fish etc. together with the vegetables – are brought to the table on one large platter, meat or ashette type dish. It is far speedier to hand round one such object as opposed to dealing with a procession of bowls and there is a much better chance of food that is intended to be hot remaining so. Duck, chicken or pigeon breasts, rack of lamb or fillet of beef – all swiftly sliced – or fillets of fish and individual game birds such as partridge or quail are ideal whilst casseroles, daubes and stews as well as savoury pies – 'One Pot Dishes' – are also obvious candidates. If, however, you do decide on a large joint of meat, then make sure you have a skilful carver to hand and arm them with a sharpened knife! Similarly, if you do not have another half to be barman then appoint one guest on arrival to do this and put them in charge of the drinks department having set everything ready on a small side table, including a bottle opener and ice bucket.

Finally, do avoid spending half the evening with your hands in the sink. Guests who are forced to watch their host clattering away continuously soaping plates, cutlery and glassware are indeed entitled to wonder how much their own presence is valued. This is the one and only department where I draw the line at offers, however kind and well-intentioned, of any form of help. I prefer to do this bit in my own time after everyone has departed and, similarly, when in someone else's home never feel remotely guilty about not offering to don the Marigolds and plunge them into the sink.

Having sorted out the actual dinner, it is worth spending a little time and consideration on the setting. Style means all and, reassuringly for the vast majority of us, this has nothing whatsoever do with money. People can entertain on all types of budget and in all sorts of different surroundings and it does not necessarily follow that the most lavish settings are the best. Often, snug squashed up gatherings can have far more allure and atmosphere than a rigidly formal occasion which lacks any type of warmth or ambience. True style, as we well know, comes from within and is all about creating something from nothing.

Whether lunch, supper or dinner are to take place in a dining room, kitchen, hallway, loft conversion, cellar, conservatory or indeed outside on a balcony, in a gazebo or in the environs of the garden itself – it is wise to take into account the basic comforts of one's guests. First consideration must be the room temperature or, if outdoors, suitable shading from heat and sun when appropriate. In chillsome conditions, nothing is more cheering than a blazing log fire which creates a homely feeling of warmth and cosiness. Of course, it's not always easy to gauge the temperature correctly as everyone tends to have a different thermostat but, ideally, I would avoid placing the larger and hence better insulated of one's friends slap up against a searing radiator.

Lighting is another critical factor which can make or mar a party. Natural daylight is wonderful providing it is not streaming in so strongly as to bedazzle people's eyes, in which case blinds or partially drawn curtains become a blessing. After dark it is just as important. Blazing overhead and searching spotlights should be avoided at all costs. The penetrating glare of a high watt bulb always puts me so on edge whereas soft sympathetic lighting is far more soothing. Lanterns and hurricane lamps too possess a rustic romantic charm of their own whilst candlelit rooms can work miracles when enhancing feminine beauty to its bewitching best!

And whilst on the subject of candles, those stored in the deep-freeze prior to use burn more slowly, increasing their longevity. Scented candles lend their own carefully crafted aromas to a room and are also a useful method of removing that lingering smell of cigarette and cigar smoke whilst a bowl of vinegar left out overnight is another effective, if less sweetly smelling, panacea. Don't forget also, to save orange skins from which the juice has been squeezed. Dry them out slowly in the oven or Aga, then throw them on the fire where they will exude a wonderful fragrance. Bowls of pot-pourri are also good to have in the house though do remember that once they lose their freshness, so they lose their potency.

Comfort must also be extended to include the types of chair upon which guests are expected to sit for several hours. No one expects to be seated in splendour on the finest antique mahogany carver but it is wise to invest in something moderately accommodating. Even an ordinary kitchen or garden chair, when equipped with a cushion or pad, is perfectly acceptable. Not being blessed with much cover on my backside, I am always very conscious of not seating people on something unbearably firm, hence seats with as much 'give' in them as a sheet of welded steel are best avoided. Equally sensible – take the precaution not to place the better upholstered of one's friends on the spindliest chairs you possess unless, of course, you are short of firewood! Personally I like those high back chairs which can be made up at reasonable cost though my own collection of seats is unmatched and not colour-coded. Their only common denominator is that they are all of a complementary height to one another. Nothing is worse than scarcely being able to squeeze your legs beneath or sitting with your chin on the table because the chairs are in the wrong proportion to it.

The choice of china available today is limitless and ranges from the finest porcelain right across the spectrum to individually crafted pottery. Whilst of course it is a luxury to have a beautifully matched set of china, it is by no means essential. I like to scour antique and bric-a-brac shops for bits and bobs and over the years have collected a whole array of blue and white china which, though individually all vaguely different, looks charming together. Provided these oddments are linked in some way, either through colour or pattern, then the mix'n'match route is not only an economical but also a most attractive option. For puddings and cheese I like to introduce something completely different. Large coloured glass plates, for example, look wacky and chic, as do square or rectangular plates.

When it comes to selecting glassware, there are designs to please every conceivable taste. Nowadays, I veer towards using a fairly plain variety made of clear, thin bevelled glass simply because they are the nicest to drink from. They should have a decent length of stem and a reasonably sized round bowl that tapers towards the rim – a tulip shape is ideal, so that the wine may be swirled around without spillage and the bouquet still captured.

Tables look wonderful when dressed with coloured wine glasses though serious oenophiles can become exercised about imbibing their beloved nectars from such vessels maintaining it can mar the taste. Indeed many wine merchants sell what they consider to be the crème de la crème collection of glasses from which to drink an infinite variety of wines. These are called Riedl and come from Austria. Ideally, use two wine glasses – one for red which should be the larger of the two, and the other for white. I like to have a different style of water glass which acts as a contrast. I favour chunky tumblers and have some in a rich mulberry which go well with a Cranberry-coloured, twisted barley pattern water jug I found in a junk yard. For real pizzazz, I sometimes add a few ice cubes containing redcurrants to this. Small Moroccan or Indian tea glasses, bound with gold rims, and which come in an assortment of colours are another attractive option for the water.

Since the table is generally regarded as the showpiece of any party it deserves to be beautifully presented. Whether it is bedecked with a cloth or not is surely dependent upon what type of surface we are talking about. Generally speaking though, the more workmanlike its appearance, the prettier it will look when covered. A well polished mahogany table, on the other hand, makes a great backdrop to gleaming cutlery, sparkling glass and silverware. Glass and mirror-topped tables are very sophisticated providing there are no smudgy fingerprints in evidence! Raid local markets, brocante shops and private house sales for heavy duty damask napkins which can be picked up remarkably cheaply, largely because many people are put-off by the thought of laundering them. Don't be – they make the purchase of those more superior paper napkins seem very extravagant by comparison. And for special occasions, I might roll these up cigarette fashion, tie them with pretty ribbon or coloured raffia and, for that extra something, tuck a handwritten placecard or fresh flower inside. Old linen cloths are another easy-to-come-by treasure and when these are not large enough to cover the entire table surface, then lay them over a large plain white sheet. And, if you need the same cloth for the following day and there is not time to wash it, then simply turn it over to hide any stains! This is not the only option, however, so don't feel constrained to bow to the bog standard sort – there are plenty of alternative materials to choose from – a thick woollen rug from a Scottish mill (though do put something suitable underneath to stop it from sliding around), kelim type rugs and even lengths of gaudily coloured saris.

Cutlery comes in all manner of styles. From huge canteens of hallmarked heirlooms passed down through the generations to modern, contemporary designs – the world's your oyster. Don't forget however, once again, to rummage round antique centres for bundles of forks, spoons and bone-handled knives which are virtually given away.

Silver always looks lovely on the table especially when it has been polished to perfection. Perhaps a large rosebowl, trophy or cup may be used as a centrepiece whilst smaller decorative items, such as butter and bon-bon dishes, salt cellars and pepper mills, wine coasters, ashtrays, as well as ornamental birds and animals all lend their own note of glamour. Just make sure all is gleaming as a result of frequent contact with the silverdip, however dull a chore this is! Those brown-tinged fork tines are a bit of a giveaway!

Finally, flowers. Wherever and whenever possible, I raid the countryside hedgerows and verges for wild blooms, foliage and greenery, hips and berries which means that one can often get away without spending money actually buying flowers – however gorgeously tempting these often are! The time I really weaken is when I am unable to resist great armfuls of parrot tulips which freefall in tumbling, carefree cascades out of their respective vases in a wonderfully chaotic yet splashy show. Those aside, catkins, pussy and twisted willow twigs, spring daffodils and bulbs, rhododendrons, arched boughs of blossom, lily of the valley and stems of lilac, cow parsley – its delicate lacy mop heads, alchemilla mollis from the garden path, syringa (Mexican orange blossom), honeysuckle and branches of buddleia all take their turn at my table as each one makes its annual appearance. Then, as summer progresses, the herbaceous borders burst forth and can be raided for scented stocks, peonies, roses, sweet peas, delphiniums, daisies and cosmos – all of which all epitomise the beauty of an authentic English garden.

There are any number of different containers, pots and baskets in which to put flowers and many of these respond mercifully well to 'grip and drop' or even 'plonk' methods of arrangement. What, for example, could be easier than a single stem such as a pink Neroli lily in a narrow-sided water glass and then to place these either in a long row down the length of the table or put one in front of each person's place? Good old fashioned china jugs, ancient soup tureens, and teapots, tin, metal and enamelled buckets are all easy to fill. Lately I have taken a tip from Nigel Slater who plants up his fish kettle with bulbs. Trendsetters may prefer to resort to that pair of shoes, too high to totter in! Just line the feet with cellophane paper then wedge in a soaked oasis and fill with flowers. And for something larger to stand, perhaps, either side of a doorway – go for stout farmyard milk churns which look great stuffed with armfuls of sunflowers. When using flowers on the table itself, think of height. Veer towards something that is either very low or else extremely high. That way, there is no danger of these blocking people's view of one another when seated, though I concede there have been moments and times when such an obstruction might have been rather welcome as well as appropriate! Lily vases are a good investment and I fill the bases of these with seashells, empty snail shells or glass marbles then top with tall arched wands of flowers. Pay heed, when using any sort or shape of glass vessel to ensure these are clean. A spot of bleach in the water can do wonders here and an old wives' tale advocates adding a dash of lemonade to make flowers last that much longer whilst the expert florist relies on iodised water!

Orthodox presentation or that touch of witty light-hearted individualism – it matters not. Ring the changes – something fun and funky is always a good talking point. Plain glass or perspex round bowls containing a few jolly goldfish and topped with a water lily or two are inexpensive and striking. So, too, are heads of vivid hydrangeas immersed in tall cylindrical vases filled with same-coloured water (use those tiny bottles of artificial food colouring!). Orchids as well are fabulous in this way. Similarly, heads of flowers floating on the surface of a large bowl of water make another stunning spectacle and are an inspired way of dealing with blooms which drop their pollen everywhere – e.g. hellebores such as Christmas Roses.

Bright fruits and vegetables should not be ignored either. Day-glo oranges, especially blood, or rosy red apples submerged in the bottom of clear glass vases then speared with swathes of foliage and hips to anchor them look ace as does a clear square container packed with a mixture of limes, lemons and kumquats (no liquid necessary for them!). A vast pyramid of strawberries, stalks intact, on a large platter is a mouth-watering table piece. Look, also, to the kitchen garden for inspiration as the Elizabethans did with their great 'sallet' displays. Globe artichokes, gleaming aubergines and courgettes; squashes and gourds packed into long shallow baskets or trugs make a departure from the usual. As do miniature pots planted up with lollorosso lettuces, ornamental cabbages and herbs such as rosemary, thyme and golden oregano or, at the opposite end of the scale, great wispy fronds of fennel. Alternatively, amass a pile of large seashells on a pretty plate – good for a fishy theme.

For that 'Blue Peter' touch, venture into the woods and country lanes to gather wayside pheasant tail feathers (if the entire casualty is there for the taking then rush it home for the pot!), fir cones as well as some winter greenery such as fern branches. Then stick these plus the plumage into oasis and surround with the cones and quails' eggs. This makes a fun display for shooting lunches and dinners and once again, everything is for free.

So – arm yourself with a basket, a pair of secateurs and step outside to see what you can find …

Soups, Starters and Salads

Soups

Whenever the word 'soup' is mentioned I always think of that wonderful line from Lewis Carroll's *Alice in Wonderland*, 'Soup, soup of the evening, beautiful soup.' To me, there is nothing more comforting than a bowl of soup though do make sure it is a bowl and not a bucket if it is to be served as a first course – otherwise the latter can fill one up far too quickly for what is to follow.

I love the different dimensions and characteristics a soup may assume. Thick, chunky, rustic elixirs and broths, all steaming hot in winter are followed by iced soups for sizzling summer days, sometimes set to a jellied consistency or thin consommé-style liquids – and all in a bewitching array of colours. Think cool, verdant green pea and mint or velvet smooth veloutés with juicy pink prawns floating on their surface for the summer season, marvellous maroon Borscht topped with a spoonful of crème fraîche mixed with horse-radish and a snowstorm of chives for Christmas celebrations.

The most important thing to remember about soup is that it is not a repository for whatever leftovers the fridge and pantry may contain. Forget limp carrots, aging potatoes sprouting shoots and other wrinkled relics from the back of the rack which render that old chestnut 'Cream of Vegetable Soup' a heart-sinking and dismal concoction. Concentrate, instead, on selecting only zingingly fresh ingredients which will taste precisely of their composition. For this reason, I have given up using my lovingly home-made chicken stock when creating soups. Its rich, concentrated flavour is wasted on these occasions when a stock cube, either chicken or vegetable, will suffice admirably though do be careful when seasoning as commercial brands tend to be quite salty.

Parsley Potager

I often feel sorry for parsley. After all, how many times does one read at the end of a recipe, 'Decorate with parsley'? It's as if it is destined only ever to be the bridesmaid and never the bride. This is quite wrong. Try this soup and see for yourself.

1 medium onion, peeled and finely chopped

1 large potato, peeled and diced

Large bunch freshly picked parsley (flat leaf or curly) – separate leaves from stalks and keep both

570 ml (1 pint) chicken or veg stock (I use a cube)

Crème fraîche or double cream – optional

Seasoning

Begin by cooking the onion in a little of the stock, covering the pan with a lid, until soft and translucent. Just make sure you add a little more liquid if required to prevent the onion from 'catching'. After about 10 minutes add the diced potatoes and parsley stalks tied in a bunch with string, and continue to cook, adding a little of the made-up stock.

When these ingredients are cooked through, pour in some more liquid, bring to the boil and plunge in the parsley heads. As soon as these are limp, remove from the heat to retain their colour. Fish out the stalks and discard then process the soup either in a liquidiser or with an electric stick, until smooth.

Season to taste and add the crème fraîche if using. This may be served either reheated or chilled.

Tip from the Sink ~

Garnish this with a blob of parsley pesto, crème fraîche mixed with chopped parsley leaves, or croutons.

Celeriac and Celery

1 medium onion, peeled and finely diced

Olive oil

1 head celery, leaves removed and reserved, stalks finely chopped

1 bulb celeriac, peeled and cut into chunks

750 ml (1¼ pints) light stock

Pepper and celery salt

Sauté the onion in the olive oil until soft then add some stock and the celery and celeriac. Cover with a lid and cook until the vegetables are done. Remove from the heat and liquidise, adding more liquid as necessary and the seasoning. For a velvet smooth finish, pass through a sieve and finish with a swirl of cream and top each bowl with a few of the celery leaves.

Tips from the Sink ～

- *Try adding a few shredded leaves of wild garlic when in season to give the soup that extra bite.*

- *Melt in some Stilton cheese – good when there are Christmas leftovers.*

Soups, Starters and Salads

Jerusalem Artichoke and Cannellini Bean

The inclusion of the beans is a means of subtly tempering the full strength (and characteristics) of this vegetable!

450 g (1 lb) Jerusalem artichokes, scrubbed and peeled	Vanilla pod, split lengthways and seeds scraped out
1 x 300 g (12 oz) tin cannellini beans, rinsed in cold water and drained	1 litre (1¾ pints) chicken or veg stock
Olive oil	Crème fraîche or double cream
1 medium onion, peeled and finely diced	Grated nutmeg
	Seasoning

Drop the peeled artichokes into a bowl of acidulated water to prevent discolourisation. Heat the olive oil in a saucepan and gently sauté the onion until soft but not coloured. Add the artichokes, vanilla seeds and a little of the stock, cover with a lid and cook until the chokes are soft. Spoon in the beans and blitz to a smooth consistency, pouring on more stock as necessary. Add seasoning, nutmeg and crème fraîche as desired.

Garnishes might include

Truffle oil mixed with a little cream

Vacuum-sealed chestnuts, finely diced and sautéed in butter until crisp

Cooked girolle or other mushrooms

Snippets of bacon or a piece of baked Parma ham

A ladle of moules marinière or seared scallops

Tip from the Sink ～

Acidulated water has a few drops of lemon juice added to it though chefs often use Vitamin C powder, available from chemists.

French Onion Soup

This is a real hot-shot amongst winter soups and an out-and-out favourite of mine. The true flavour of the onions is highlighted by slow, patient cooking which accentuates their natural sweetness.

6 or 7 large onions, peeled and thinly sliced in rounds

50 g (2 oz) butter

1 bouquet garni (leek, parsley stalks, thyme and bay leaf tied together)

1 tablespoon soft brown sugar

750 ml (1¼ pints) chicken stock

300 ml (½ pint) cider

Double cream

Seasoning and freshly grated nutmeg

French baguette, cut into diagonal slices and lightly toasted

Grated Gruyère cheese

Begin by melting the butter then add the onions and bouquet garni, cover with a lid and leave to cook very gently without allowing them to take on any colour. After approx 10 minutes, add the sugar and a little of the stock, cover again, and continue to cook. This process takes at least 30 minutes as you want to end up with very soft, sweet-flavoured onions. Add more stock, the cider and cream, then the seasoning and a generous rasping of nutmeg. Pile the slices of baguette with the cheese and place under a hot grill until the cheese has melted and is nicely browned. Ladle the hot soup into bowls and top each one with a croûte.

Tips from the Sink ～

• *Liquidise this soup until completely smooth. Transfer to preheated thermos flasks. It makes a brilliant shooting day's elevenses.*

• *Equally good, also, is to replace the cider with Calvados to taste.*

Smoked Haddock and Saffron

450 g (1 lb) smoked haddock, undyed	Olive oil
600 ml (1 pint) milk	Bay leaf
1 onion, peeled and finely chopped	Strands saffron
1 leek, sliced	Pepper
1 potato, peeled and diced	Flat leaf parsley, chopped

Begin by heating the milk in a pan with the bay leaf and a pinch of the saffron threads. When hot, add the fish and poach gently for approx 4 minutes – so it is still a little under-done. Remove the fish from the liquid and set both aside. In another pan, cook the onion in a little olive oil until it begins to soften then add the leek and, after a few more minutes, the potato. Pour in the fishy milk and simmer gently until everything is done. To finish, flake the fish and add to the pan, remove the bay leaf then purée to a smooth consistency. Add pepper though you will not need salt as the haddock is smoked. Add a little more milk/water if it is too thick and sprinkle with the parsley.

Tips from the Sink ~

Vary this soup in the following ways:

- *Do not bother to blend but leave everything in chunks.*

- *For supper in a bowl, add a tin of drained sweetcorn, cooked fennel, prawns, mussels or snippets of crispy bacon and top with a poached egg.*

- *Include a splash of white wine, Noilly Prat or Pernod.*

Borscht and Cranberry Soup

The alliance of beets and cranberries is to be recommended.

1 bunch beetroot, washed and trimmed,
    chopped up small
Olive oil
1 red onion, peeled and diced
100 g (4 oz) fresh cranberries
2 glasses cranberry juice

600 ml (1 pint) chicken stock or can
    consommé soup and water
Lemon juice and seasoning
Crème fraîche mixed with horseradish
    sauce to taste
Scissored chives

Begin by placing the chunks of beetroot on a large sheet of tin foil and generously anoint with olive oil, season and loosely seal. Cook in a hot oven – 200°C 400°F/Gas Mark 6 – for at least 40 minutes or until soft. Next, sauté the onion in a saucepan containing some more olive oil until just translucent then tip in the cranberries, the stock and the cranberry juice and bring gently to the boil, then simmer for a few minutes. Purée in batches together with the beets, season and add lemon juice and adjust consistency if necessary. Pass through a sieve if wished and reheat before ladling into warmed bowls. Decorate with a spoonful of the crème fraîche mix and scatter over some chives.

Tips from the Sink ～

- *Use orange, in place of the cranberry, juice.*

- *Take out a spoonful of the purée before it is too run down with the stock and mix with the crème fraîche and horseradish to use as a dip.*

Speedy Summer Gazpacho

2 x 300 ml (½ pint) bottles V8, tomato juice or Clamato

2 cucumbers, peeled, seeded and finely diced

Celery salt

Few shakes Worcester sauce

Handful mint leaves, chopped

½ cup French dressing

Snipped chives

Author's note: Cup is an American type of measure – they are sold in 'sets' of ¼, ½ and whole sizes, and are quite commonplace here in kitchen shops. A whole cup is 250 ml, half a cup is 125 ml.

Process the cucumbers with the tomato juice, Worcester sauce, seasoning, celery salt and mint. Stir in the French dressing and refrigerate until well chilled. Ladle into bowls which have also been in the fridge. Garnish with snipped chives.

Tips from the Sink ∼

- *Try adding vodka and/or sherry to this to make a Blooded Gazpacho.*

- *Set it in a ring mould to a jelly with leaf gelatine then turn out and fill the centre with watercress and chopped tomatoes.*

Avocado Soup with Prawns

With its pale pistachio colour, this makes an unbeatable no-cook summer soup.

1 carton/tub ready-made leek and potato/vichyssoise soup	Juice of a lemon
2 ripe avocados – peeled, stoned and chopped	2–3 tablespoons crème fraîche
	Seasoning
	Shelled prawns to decorate

Simply liquidise together the soup with the avocados. Add the lemon juice, crème fraîche and seasoning and, if necessary, thin down with a little cold water. Decorate with the prawns and a swirl of cream.

Tip from the Sink ∼

To pour cream onto the surface of a soup, pierce a hole in the foil lid of a tub of single cream and, squeezing the sides gently, pour round in a circle.

Shellfish Bisque

A really good bisque should linger not only in the mouth with its sweet, rich flavours but also in the mind for sheer, undiluted luxury. I make mine from cooked lobsters and crabs – usually after someone has had a party and I have begged a doggy bag of the used shells before they are thrown in the dustbin. If you do likewise make sure, however, you add the meats, from either a whole lobster or crab. (If the latter, both brown and white.) In their absence, use some juicy shelled prawns or langoustines.

3 empty lobster shells and same of crab or
   6 of one variety

Cooked meat from one lobster or crab

Bouquet garni

Olive oil

3 banana shallots or 1 onion, peeled and
   chopped

3 celery stalks, ends trimmed and finely
   chopped

2 trimmed and cleaned leeks, white parts
   only, sliced

2 carrots, peeled and roughly chopped

400 g (14 oz) tin of plum tomatoes

Large glass of white wine

300 ml (½ pint) water, light chicken or fish
   stock

150 ml (5 fl oz) double cream

Juice of ½ a lemon

Whisper of cognac or brandy

Seasoning

Begin by removing the meat from the lobster/crab and setting aside then, using a hammer, bash all empty crustacean shells into pieces and pile these into a large pan. Cover with cold water, add a bouquet garni and bring to the boil then simmer gently for 25–30 minutes. Remove from the heat, discard the shells by passing the liquid through a sieve, pressing down well on the solids to squeeze out every morsel of flavour, and leave this to cool together with the bouquet garni.

Next, heat a little olive oil in a pan and sauté the shallots/onions until soft and translucent then add the celery, leeks and carrots plus a little of the reserved shell stock and cook these until soft. Tip in the tomatoes, some more stock and the white wine and bring back to the boil. Fish out the bouquet garni, and process in batches until smooth. Adjust consistency by adding more stock as necessary, pass through a sieve if wished, and return to the pan. Add the lemon juice, cream, seasoning and finally the brandy or cognac and the reserved meat then heat through until piping hot and serve at once.

Tip from the Sink ～

The secret of a really good bisque is not to drown out the flavour with an overdose of cognac or brandy. It was Simon Hopkinson who advocated the use of only a 'whisper' of this alcohol and herein lies the secret of this most deliciously subtle treat.

Curried Parsnip and Apple with Hazelnut Pesto

This is very much a winter soup with the undertone of the curry powder adding a pleasing warmth to the end result.

350 g (12 oz) parsnips, peeled, trimmed and chopped
1 medium onion, peeled and finely diced
2–3 Cox's apples, peeled, cored and sliced
Generous pinch of curry powder

900 ml (1½ pints) of chicken or vegetable stock
Seasoning
Crème fraîche

Toss the onion into a pan with a little of the stock, cover with a lid and cook until soft, making sure the onion does not catch and start to burn. When done, add the parsnips, apples and a pinch of curry powder and pour on some more stock. Continue to cook until everything is soft then whiz in the processor until smooth, adding more liquid as required. Return to the pan, season as necessary and taste. Stir in some crème fraîche and reheat to serve.

Hazelnut Pesto

3 tablespoons hazelnuts, lightly toasted and skins removed
large bunch flat leaf parsley, leaves only

100 ml/4 fl oz olive oil
seasoning

First, wrap the hazelnuts in a teatowel and rub to remove paper skins. Discard these and place nuts and parsley in a food processor then whizz to a paste. Run down to a purée with the olive oil and season.

Tip from the Sink ∼

Remember that the flavour of the curry powder will develop and strengthen so don't be too heavy-handed initially. Another pinch may always be added at a later stage – it's more difficult to tone down a searing spiciness!

Bullshot

Traditionally fashioned from oxtail bones, my version is less orthodox but far speedier and does not appear to suffer unduly laced, as it is, with both vodka and sherry. It is wonderfully fortifying for anyone attempting to ward off cold, wet weather!

2 tins consommé – I use Waitrose's own brand	Generous measure each of sherry and vodka
Shake of Worcester sauce	Twist of pepper

Very simply, heat the consommé until boiling, add the Worcester sauce followed by the alcohol – exactly how much is entirely down to you – and pepper then swiftly transfer to a preheated thermos.

Tip from the Sink ∼

Remember that boiling reduces the strength of alcohol. By adding it at the last minute it retains its potency.

Starters

These set the tone for what follows. Ideally, starters should merely whet the appetite, stir up the gastric juices and thereby tempt and tantalise the diner so that they can look forward to the main course with keen anticipation. Nothing dampens the spirits faster than a first course so bucolically rich and filling that it leaves one reaching for an Alka-Seltzer.

Jellied Beetroot with Prawns

1 bunch fresh beetroot	Drop or two balsamic vinegar
110 ml (4 fl oz) cranberry juice	Lemon juice
7 whole leaves gelatine	Seasoning
250 g (8 oz) shelled prawns	

Line a one-litre/1¾ pint terrine tin with cling-film – this sticks better if you first brush the sides and base with a little oil. Leave plenty of overhang. Scrub and trim the beetroot – no need to peel – and chop up roughly then cook in boiling water until soft. Drain and reserve 3–4 tablespoons of the cooking liquid. Purée with the cranberry juice and some of the cooking liquid so it is quite slushy and push through a sieve. Meanwhile, steep the gelatine leaves in a bowl of ice cold water and leave for at least 10 minutes until completely soft. Season the beets and add the lemon juice and balsamic vinegar to taste.

When the gelatine is ready, squeeze out the excess water and put in a saucepan to melt or leave it to stand on the side of the Aga in a bowl. When liquid, stir into the beetroot mixture. To assemble, cover the base of the tin with some of the purple mixture and dot in some prawns. Put in the fridge to set, then repeat building up the terrine layer by layer. In this way, the prawns do not all sink to the base. When completed, gently fold the cling-film over the top and leave in the fridge for at least six hours.

To serve, turn out on to a board and arrange a slice on individual plates. Crème fraîche mixed with horseradish is excellent with this or you could turn it into a summer main course with new potato and smoked eel salad.

Tip from the Sink 〜

Variation: Reserve a couple of the beetroot, peel off their skins and dice up finely then add to the terrine in place of the prawns.

Chicken Liver Parfait

Unctuously smooth, this transforms the humble chicken liver into something special. Good as a starter or as part of a picnic or buffet. Make at least a day before serving to maximise flavours. Onion marmalade, fruit chutney or jelly as well as Cumberland sauce are all ideal with it. I have made it including a clove of crushed garlic but prefer it without. Up to you.

450 g (1 lb) chicken livers
1 tablespoon redcurrant (or similar) jelly, melted
150 ml (¼ pint) chicken stock

3 eggs
600 ml (1 pint) double cream
Rasping nutmeg
Seasoning

Preheat the oven to 160°C/325°F/gas mark 3. Brush the insides of a 1 litre (1¾ pint) capacity terrine or loaf tin with oil then line with cling-film. Soak the chicken livers in milk for half an hour to remove any traces of bitterness. Drain and remove any sinews then transfer to a food processor and whiz together with the jelly then pour on the chicken stock. Next, add the eggs followed by the cream. Season with salt, pepper and the nutmeg. Pass the mixture through a fine sieve then pour into the terrine tin and cover the top with a double layer of greaseproof paper. Stand this in a bain-marie and cook for approx an hour until the parfait is just starting to set but still slightly wobbly remembering that it will continue to cook once removed from the oven as it cools. Remove from the oven and the bain-marie and leave until completely cold before refrigerating.

To serve, unmould onto a chopping board and dip the blade of a sharp knife into a jug of boiling water before cutting each slice. Toasted brioche is delicious with this.

Tip from the Sink ~

When making terrines and parfaits always use the salt and pepper mills more generously than you might imagine you need to. Somehow the cooking process necessitates a higher level of seasoning.

Griddled Asparagus with Curried Mayonnaise

'The Greeks ate it wild, Louis XIV built banquets around it while the Victorians virtually outlawed it from polite society.'

More fool them, I say. The English asparagus season is but a short one so make the maximum of this most decadent of vegetables whilst you can. Whether steamed or cooked in lightly salted boiling water and eaten with melted butter or with a host of other ingredients, it never loses its allure amongst its myriad worshippers. I like to griddle it when the combination of the almost-smoked and slightly charred (no more!) flavour of the spears is extra delicious and very easy to cook.

> 1 kg (2 lbs) asparagus, trimmed
> Olive oil
> Sea salt

Heat a little olive oil in a ridged griddle pan (use a frying pan if you don't have one) and then add the trimmed asparagus and scatter over some sea salt. Serve it straight, add it to salads or accompany it with a bowl of home-made mayonnaise to which a pinch or two of curry powder and a generous dollop of crème fraîche have been added. The hint of curry powder is barely discernible but lends a certain je ne sais quoi.

Tip from the Sink ～

When preparing asparagus snap off the woody stalks. The point of doing this is that each one will automatically break off in the 'right' place thereby simplifying the cook's decision as to where, precisely, it should be cut.

Spinach Soufflé with Anchovy Sauce

Nothing beats a soufflé for visual effect providing, of course, it rises. That said, a soufflé is about far more than just a lot of fluffed-up egg whites. It also needs heart and substance so don't be too alarmed if yours doesn't scale skyscraper heights. And remember, contrary to widespread belief, soufflés can be prepped several hours in advance and left in the fridge until you are ready to cook them. I always make mine in individual (though generously sized) ramekins and, if there is any mixture left over, cook a spare one. Unless you have a fan oven, the heat is not always evenly distributed so sometimes you may find one does not rise as well as the others.

100 g (4 oz) fresh baby spinach leaves	*For the Sauce*
50 g (2 oz) butter	3 egg yolks
40 g (1½ oz) plain flour	1 tablespoon water
300 ml (½ pint) milk	175 g (6 oz) butter, melted
5 eggs, separated	Squeeze lemon juice
Grated nutmeg	Small tin anchovy fillets
Seasoning	

To prepare the soufflé, butter individual ramekins and stand in the fridge. Rinse the spinach leaves in cold water, shake off the excess and cook quickly in a pan on the stove until just wilted. Strain and squeeze out all the liquid then chop finely.

Melt the butter in a saucepan, stir in the flour to form a thick roux then whisk in the milk gradually until all is smooth. Add the nutmeg and seasoning. Leave to cool for a few minutes then beat in the egg yolks.

Whisk the egg whites in a separate bowl until stiff but not too dry (if you beat them too hard they cannot rise as effectively) then, using a large metal spoon, mix one spoonful into the spinach ingredients then lightly fold in the remaining egg whites. Turn into the ramekin dishes, stand all on a baking sheet and return to the fridge.

To cook the soufflés, preheat the oven to 180°C/350°F/gas mark 4 and when hot, slide them in on the tray and leave to cook for approx 10–12 minutes until risen and golden brown.

For the sauce, combine the egg yolks with the water in a pan and cook over a gentle heat, whisking continuously. Stir in the melted butter and add the squeeze of lemon juice. Blend the anchovies with a little water in the processor until smooth then add to the saucepan with the eggs and butter and pass through a sieve.

To serve, place the soufflés on saucers and bring to the table immediately with the sauce in a jug. Spear a hole in the top and pour in the sauce.

Tip from the Sink ~

Warning shots about not opening the oven door whilst cooking a soufflé are – if you will excuse the pun – a load of hot air. After all, if like me you cook in an Aga, what should you do – drill a hole through the enamel door?! Just make sure there isn't a howling draft blowing in through the window, then open and shut the door very gently when having a peek.

Warm Mushroom Mousses

These are wonderfully elegant and a doddle to make. They are also an excellent accompaniment to fillet of beef and roast partridge – along with the Mushroom and Madeira Sauce.

450 g (1 lb) mixed mushrooms
Olive oil
300 ml (½ pint) double cream
Handful flat leaf parsley leaves, chopped
Lemon juice
2 eggs
Seasoning

For the Mushroom and Madeira Sauce
175 g (6 oz) mixed mushrooms, cleaned,
   sliced and gently sautéed in butter
300 ml (½ pint) jellied stock
½ tablespoon redcurrant jelly
50 g (2 oz) cold butter, cubed
Madeira to taste
Seasoning
Squeeze lemon juice

To make the mousses preheat the oven to 180°C/350°F/gas mark 4. Sauté the mushrooms in a frying pan with a little olive oil until soft. Reserve a few for the sauce and put the rest in the processor with the double cream, parsley, seasoning, lemon juice and eggs and blitz to a smooth puree. Taste for flavour. Transfer the mixture into individual dariole moulds or ramekins which have been lined with cling-film and stand in a roasting tin. Pour in water to come halfway up and set on top of the stove. Bring to the boil then transfer immediately to the oven and bake until just puffed up and firm to the touch – approx 15 minutes. Remove, lift out of the tin and leave to stand for 5–10 minutes until ready to serve.

To make the sauce, reduce the stock by at least half then melt in redcurrant jelly. When dissolved, add the Madeira – how much is up to you – and whisk in the cold butter to achieve a glossy sheen. Spoon in the mushrooms to warm through, season and finish with a squeeze of lemon juice. If making this in advance, you may wish to pour in a little more Madeira when reheating just to give it that extra 'edge'.

To serve, turn out the mousses onto warmed plates, decorate with a couple of parsley leaves and pour around a little of the Mushroom and Madeira sauce.

Celeriac and Jerusalem Artichoke Mousses

Celeriac may not win a beauty contest but its gnarled appearance belies a delicate flavour and its alliance with Jerusalem artichokes is a harmonious pairing. Once again, this also goes well with the Mushroom and Madeira Sauce and, baked in one large ovenproof dish, it is especially good alongside a roast rib of beef for Sunday lunch when the above sauce could, for a change, replace the standard gravy!

1 medium celeriac, peeled and roughly chopped	150 ml (5 fl oz) double cream
450 g (1 lb) Jerusalem artichokes, peeled and chopped	3 eggs
	1 teaspoon creamed horseradish
	Celery salt and pepper

Preheat the oven to 180°C/350°F/gas mark 4. Paint individual moulds with a little sunflower oil and line each one with cling-film.

Boil the celeriac and artichokes in a pan of water to which a few drops of lemon juice have been added until completely tender, then drain.

Purée the vegetables together very thoroughly with the cream, eggs and horseradish, then season and pass through a sieve.

Fill the moulds with the mixture, tapping each one on a worktop to remove any pockets of air, then place in a roasting tin half filled with warm water. Place in the oven and bake until just set – this should take around 20–25 minutes. Remove from the oven and the roasting tin and leave to stand.

Tip from the Sink ～

When selecting Jerusalem artichokes, rifle through them very carefully and choose the least knobbly ones – these are far easier to peel! That said, growers of this vegetable now seem to be producing smoother-skinned tubers.

Cetinale Game Terrine

Easter for RA and me was routinely spent in the Var region of France staying with friends. These visits were cherished for the majestic surroundings, magical weather and memorable company. Crackling log fires lit each morning at dawn whilst we slumbered upstairs unaware of such toil greeted us when we (eventually!) descended for breakfast to make plans for the day ahead. Games of boules; walks through the hills carpeted with spring's wild flowers; leisurely sun-drenched outdoor lunches washed down with wines from the surrounding vineyards; the luxury of curling up and reading a book under a shady grape arbour; a dip in the stone-lined 'basins' filled with their icy cold gin clear waters which ran straight off the mountains; moulding clay in our host's pottery shed; raids on the local markets laden with their irresistible and opulent array of new season's fruit, vegetables and flowers – all these delights were surpassed only by the exquisite cooking of Ricard the chef. And, as is the way of these things when food lovers are gathered together, talk invariably turned to matters of, well, just food itself. Fond memories of happy days and happy times are revived each time I make this recipe given to me by Claire Ward – fellow house guest. I have named it in honour of her lovely Tuscan villa. It became a firm fixture for Saturday lunches back at Hill Farm along with baked potatoes, a green salad and some crusty bread. It tastes best if prepared a few days in advance – that way the flavours can develop. Vary it according to what is available.

SERVES 8

675 g (1½ lbs) minced belly of pork

225 g (8 oz) chicken livers, sinews removed

2 onions, finely chopped

50 g (2 oz) butter

Plump clove garlic, finely chopped

1 egg

2 large tablespoons Cognac or brandy

Seasoning

1 tablespoon each fresh thyme and parsley leaves

Grated nutmeg

100 g (4 oz) toasted hazelnuts, skins rubbed off, or shelled pistachios

175 g (6 oz) presoaked pitted prunes or apricots

Prosciutto or bacon rashers (rindless)

Preheat the oven to 160°C/325°F/gas mark 3. Sauté the onions and garlic in butter until soft then mix together in a large bowl with all the other ingredients making sure to err on the side of generosity with the seasoning. Line a 1.25 litre (2 pint) terrine tin with the pieces of prosciutto or bacon leaving a decent overhang then spoon in the mixture pressing down well. Fold over the ham or bacon and cover the top with a double layer of aluminium foil and place the tin in a bain-marie, half filled with hot water, and cook in the oven for 1½ hours. To check whether it is done, insert a skewer into the centre and, if it comes out clean, it is ready. Remove from the bain-marie and leave to cool. Weight and refrigerate. To serve, unmould onto a board and cut into elegant slices using a sharp knife dipped into a jug of boiling water. Accompany with either onion marmalade, Cumberland sauce, celeriac remoulade, cornichons or a fruit chutney.

Tips from the Sink ～

- Slithers of raw game, such as partridge, duck, pigeon or pheasant breasts may also be incorporated.

- If using the chicken livers, soak these in milk for a few hours beforehand to remove any traces of bitterness.

Tomato Pudding

A savoury 'take' on the traditional fruited Summer Pudding. Jillie Barrow is a near neighbour, friend and an accomplished cook. Together we can spend hours discussing food. She mentioned one day that she had seen a recipe in The Week *for the above but, hard as we both searched, neither of us could find that particular issue of the magazine. After much discussion and comparison of notes, this is my interpretation of what she described. This recipe relies on finding the ripest, sweetest, juiciest and unflawed tomatoes so, if your produce is not up to scratch, make something else.*

SERVES 8

Loaf of thinly sliced white or brown bread, crusts removed, to line a 1 litre (1¾ pint) pudding basin

300 ml (½ pint) tomato juice or passata (I used Clamato and Big Tom but whatever is to hand)

1.3 kg (3 lbs plus) of ripe, flavoursome tomatoes, peeled and chopped – I like to use several varieties including some cherry tomatoes on the vine

2 large tablespoons tomato ketchup

1 medium aubergine or courgette, cut into 5 mm slices

Good shake or three of Worcester sauce

Tabasco – to taste

1 tablespoon cider vinegar

1 teaspoon sugar

Shake celery salt

Finely chopped and seeded red chilli

Seasoning

2 tablespoons each shredded basil and marjoram leaves

Start by lining the basin with cling-film. To make sure it sticks wipe some sunflower oil around the inside first. Next pour some tomato juice into a flat dish and dip triangles of bread into it. Press these around the sides of the bowl and cut a circle for the base. Seal the joins together with your fingers so the bread glues together and there are no gaps.

Put the tomatoes and any juice from them into a pan with the tomato ketchup, Worcester sauce, Tabasco, sugar, cider vinegar, celery salt and chilli, and cook for approximately 5 minutes. Strain into a colander over a bowl and leave to cool, then mix in the herbs. Meanwhile, sauté the aubergine or courgette slices in olive oil until nicely browned then pat dry on kitchen paper. Return the tomato juices to the pan and reduce until thickened. Taste for seasoning and check it has enough flavour. If not raid the store cupboard to jazz it up – pretend you are making a Spicy Virgin Mary! – i.e. a squeeze of lemon juice, a dash of sherry, etc. Put half the tomato mixture into the bowl and spoon over half the tomato sauce. Top with the aubergines/courgettes then add the remaining fruit and juice then cover with more presoaked bread. Fold the cling-film over the top and find a plate which fits the surface area and weight it with something heavy (tins of beans or packets of butter will do well in the absence of old-fashioned weights). Refrigerate overnight.

To serve, turn out onto a large plate, decorate with basil leaves and serve with either basil oil or crème fraîche mixed with lemon zest, finely chopped cucumber flesh and more herbs.

Tomato and Basil Galette

This recipe stands and falls by the flavour of the tomato. It's a signature dish at one of my most favourite restaurants, Le Caprice, where the menu always includes a kaleidescope of seasonal goodies amonst its 'specials' and every ingredient served is always superlative. A real crowd pleaser it also looks as pretty as a picture on a plain white plate.

1 x 350 g (12 oz) packet puff pastry

5–6 good sized, ripe, flavoursome
    tomatoes, preferably vine – skinned and
    thinly sliced

Sun-dried tomato paste

Sea salt

Basil oil – made with 50 g (2 oz) torn basil
    leaves and 125 ml (4 fl oz) olive oil, a
    pinch of sugar and some sea salt

Sprigs basil

Preheat the oven to 200°C/400°F/gas mark 6. Roll out the pastry as thinly as possible and cut into circles the size of a large saucer (they will shrink when cooked). Prick the bases all over with the prongs of a fork and bake on a sheet for 10–12 minutes, turning them over halfway through to ensure pastry does not rise. If it has, beat it down again. These should be golden, crispy and as wafer slim as you can make them.

Remove and leave to cool slightly then spread the surface of each with a little of the sun-dried tomato paste and arrange the tomatoes in concentric circles. (I usually reckon on one per galette providing they are of a reasonable size.) Sprinkle with a smidgen of caster sugar (if to hand) and a good grinding of sea salt and place in the oven for approx 10–12 minutes until warmed through.

Transfer to individual plates and drizzle with a little of the basil oil dressing and finish each one with a basil leaf sprig.

Tips from the Sink ∼

- *If you don't have time to make the basil oil, simply run down some readymade pesto with olive oil.*

- *For an informal lunch make one large tart*

Prawn, Melon and Cucumber Cocktail

Retro fare – I dare you! After all, if Prawn Cocktail can enjoy a revival, then why shouldn't this little trio? With its minty vinaigrette, this is fresher by far.

225 g (8 oz) shelled fresh plump cooked
   prawns
1 cucumber, peeled, halved lengthways and
   seeded
1 ripe melon, preferably Cavaillon or
   Chanterais

Vinaigrette
Chopped mint leaves
Black pepper

Put the prawns, diced cucumber and chunks of melon in a large bowl then mix in the vinaigrette with the mint leaves and season with the black pepper. Leave to stand until ready to serve.

Serve in individual glass bowls, or ramekins.

Crab and Broad Bean Bruschetta

These also make a delicious canapé to hand around with preprandial drinks.

225 g (8 oz) cooked broad beans – double de-podded!

4 tablespoons olive oil

1 tablespoon tarragon vinegar

½ teaspoon tarragon mustard – or use plain Dijon

Seasoning

2 large ripe tomatoes, peeled, seeded and diced

1 tablespoon chopped herbs – e.g. flat-leaf parsley, dill, basil, mint

Pinch caster sugar

225–275 g (8–10 oz) freshly picked white crabmeat

4 slices thick country bread, e.g. sourdough, poilane

Mix the vinegar and mustard in a bowl and pour in the olive oil then season. Mash the broad beans with a fork until lightly crushed then add to the dressing along with the tomatoes, sugar and herbs. Finally, stir in the crabmeat. Toast the bread and pile a generous spoonful of the mixture on top of each piece. Garnish with a few more herbs and sit on a large flat platter covered with vine leaves.

Crab Tart

'Just Shellfish' is one of my 'Little Black Book' Cornish haunts. Based at Port Isaac, Jeremy and Liz Brown produce the best crab and lobster – live or cooked and dressed, that exists. Full stop. Last summer Richenda and I, having packed up the car at the end of our stay, called in for one final raid. We sat on the beach of this ancient fishing village, feasting on huge dressed crabs straight from the shell (our only implements being our fingers). They were so exquisitely fresh there was no need for the usual embellishments of mayonnaise and lemon juice. So, if that is not the true flavours of something speaking for

itself, then I am not sure what else is! Rather like the child determined to return home with a holiday souvenir, I sneaked back to buy another couple and slipped them into the cold box. The following day, I made them into this divine tart to share with friends for a supper starter.

SERVES 6–8

350 g (12 oz) shortcrust pastry – Saxby's is fine

450 g (1 lb) mixture white and brown crab meat

1 tablespoon tomato purée

Squeeze lemon juice

2 tablespoons Parmigiano cheese, finely grated

300 ml (½ pint) double cream or crème fraîche

3 eggs, separated

2 teaspoons Dijon mustard

1 tablespoon chopped fresh herbs – parsley, tarragon or basil

Seasoning

Preheat the oven to 180°C/350°F/gas mark 4. Roll out the pastry and line a 25 cm (10 inch) tin with a removable base. Prick all over with a fork and leave to chill in the fridge for 30 minutes then bake blind for approximately 15 minutes before removing the paper and beans and returning to the oven until just lightly browned all over. Remove and set aside.

For the filling, mix the crab meats in a bowl together with the tomato purée, lemon juice, cheese, cream, egg yolks, mustard, chopped herbs and seasoning. In a separate bowl, whisk the egg whites until stiff then gently fold into the crab. Pile the mixture into the pastry shell, slide the tin onto a baking sheet and bake in the oven for approximately 30–35 minutes until souffléd up and just firm to the touch. Remove and leave to stand for 10 minutes to 'set' as this makes it easier to slice.

Tip from the Sink ~

Make these in individual tartlet tins if you prefer.

Soups, Starters and Salads

DISHES WITH DASHERS • 53

Ceviche of Smoked Haddock

The point of this dish is that the lime juice 'cooks' the fish. Its clean, unfettered taste makes it immensely popular. Spoon blobs onto chicory or little gem leaves and serve as a canape too.

450 g (1 lb) undyed smoked haddock fillets, skinned and carefully boned

Zest and juice of ½ lemon and ½ lime

Few shakes Tabasco

Good squirt runny honey

1 teaspoon Dijon mustard

Chopped herbs, e.g. chives, tarragon, flat leaf parsley, dill

2 tablespoons mayonnaise or crème fraîche

Seasoning

Reduced balsamic vinegar (optional)

Few salad leaves and extra chopped herbs

Dice the fish into very small cubes – do not attempt to do this in a food processor as you will end up with a textureless mush! In a large bowl, mix together the lemon and lime zests and juices, Tabasco, honey, mustard, herbs and mayonnaise or crème fraîche then season well. Add the fish and combine all the ingredients, cover and refrigerate until required.

To serve, place a round cutter in the centre of four plates and spoon a quarter of the fish mix into each one, pressing down well. Dress the salad leaves and place a few, along with some extra chopped herbs, on top of each mound then remove the rings with the assistance of a palette knife. The juices should run out onto the plates so just dribble round a few dots of the balsamic vinegar to finish off. To gild the lily, top each ceviche with a poached quail's egg.

Green Beans with Hazelnuts

Simplicity itself – this deliciously straightforward little dish comes from Penny Barker. It is ideal before a rich main course being light and clean on the palate.

325 g (12 oz) French beans, topped and
    tailed
5 generous tablespoons crème fraîche

Quality hazelnut oil
75–100 g (3–4 oz) hazelnuts, toasted, skins
    removed and roughly chopped

Cook the beans briefly in plenty of boiling salted water until just al dente then drain and refresh immediately under cold running water. Dry off and arrange two layers on each plate, the under layer horizontally and the top layer placed over them vertically, rather like a noughts and crosses pattern. In a bowl, mix together the crème fraîche and enough hazelnut oil to achieve a spooning consistency. Spoon over the beans and scatter over the nuts.

Celeriac Remoulade with Parma Ham & Truffle Oil

If you buy the celeriac remoulade ready made, this can be a no-cook starter. And, even if you have to make your own, it is still a star turn of a few simple ingredients. Home-made mayonnaise is best but, if pressed for time, use Hellman's and add a nip of gin to it, or tubs of ready made brands found in the chiller shelves of a supermarket.

1 celeriac bulb, peeled and roughly
    chopped
5 tablespoons home-made mayonnaise
    mixed with wholegrain mustard
1 tablespoon crème fraîche or double
    cream

1 tablespoon roughly chopped flat-leaf
    parsley
4–6 slices Parma or Bayonne ham
Parmesan cheese
Truffle oil
Seasoning

Using a mandoline or a sharp knife, cut the celeriac into thin matchsticks and blanche quickly in boiling, salted water to soften, then drain and refresh under cold water. When cool, mix with the mayonnaise, crème fraîche (or cream) and parsley, then season.

Line individual moulds/ramekins with cling-film, keeping an overlap (paint the interior of containers with a little sunflower oil so it sticks) then mould each one with a piece of Parma ham. Fill with the remoulade, fold over the remaining ham followed by the excess cling-film and press down gently.

To serve, turn the moulds onto individual plates and peel off the cling-film. Top with a few flakes Parmesan cheese and a sprig of parsley and dribble round a few drops of the truffle oil.

Tip from the Sink ～

Use a potato peeler to shave off slices of the Parmesan cheese.

Salads

Modern day dining means that salads – far from being a mere little something on the side – now frequently assume 'main course' status and are the focal point of a menu. Thus they fully deserve a chapter of their own. Mercifully, those pitiful wilted brown lettuces, unpeeled cucumbers, hard-boiled eggs – their yolks surrounded with that gloomy-looking orbital grey rim – together with a viciously vinegared beetroot leeching out its purple stains, which masqueraded as 'salad', are but a distant memory. 'Rabbit food' has taken on a new meaning and the far-flung range of ingredients now incorporated enable an unending selection of scintillating salads to be served throughout the year according to whatever is in prime condition – be it game, fish, meat, vegetables as well as fruits.

The real secret of a great salad, however, is to resist the temptation to throw together a whole mélange of elements whose flavours merely suppress one another. Concentrate, instead, on combining carefully selected prime, seasonal foods with tastes that meld together without jarring yet, at the same time, provide diversity and interest with contrasting textures. Quite frequently, the making of a salad need be little more than an assembly job but, providing the ingredients used are all of the utmost freshness and premium quality, then it will not suffer in any way. There are endless winning combinations and all can happily be transformed into something substantial enough to satisfy even those who possess trencher-like appetites with the addition of, say, a poached egg or a piece of fish, meat or poultry.

Whenever possible though, avoid supermarket bags of mixed salad leaves which undergo twenty-five washes in chlorine and, more often than not by the time you have got them home, have sweated to a nasty slimy mess. Better, by far, to use an assortment, where possible, of home-grown leaves, however modest or limited the choice. In their absence, stick to good old-fashioned soft round lettuces and don't skimp. You need to allow one per person – at least – then divest it of all the outer leaves which are often rather motley and use only the hearts. If necessary, these can be plumped out with some spinach, sorrel or beetroot leaves and enhanced with some freshly picked herbs to provide a bowl of fresh, understated charm. Don't forget the wild rocket leaves which can be picked from the verges or the lush green peppery watercress which is to be found growing in the beds of many of our rivers. To serve this sort of no-nonsense salad will guarantee you the respect and applause of all those at the table.

Remember also, that the dressing can make or mar the success of a salad. The range and choice of oils and vinegars available is dazzling – elderflower and gooseberry is my new best friend and lends a certain fragrance of its own. Each one possesses different characteristics so there is endless scope for experimentation though it is wise, perhaps, to err on the side of caution and use the stronger ones judiciously lest they should mask the true identity of the salad. As a rule of thumb I find the best balance for a classic vinaigrette is three parts oil to one part vinegar and I often tweak the basic recipe by adding a specially flavoured oil to vary the end result.

You will notice that quantities for some of the salads below are deliberately vague so do not be frightened to tailor these amounts according to your own preferences. I am unerringly happy munching my way through piles of lettuce – it's a wonder in fact that nobody has ever thought to call me by that name!

Pear, Parma Ham with Goats' Cheese and Walnuts

2 large handfuls of mixed salad leaves,
    washed and dried
2 ripe pears, such as Comice, peeled and
    cored
Vinaigrette

6 slices best Parma ham
2 tubs of goats' cheese
75 g (3 oz) walnut halves, toasted
Snipped chives

Dress the salad leaves and the pears with the vinaigrette, adding a good twist of sea salt, then scatter over the Parma ham, small blobs of creamy goats' cheese and the walnuts. Finish off with a scattering of snipped chives and serve with walnut bread.

Tips from the Sink ～

Ingredients for this may be varied according to what is in season. For example, replace the pear with roasted beetroot when this is available. Rashers of bacon may also be substituted for the Parma ham.

Warm Pigeon Salad with Roasted Beetroot and Walnut Vinaigrette

2–3 medium beets, cleaned and diced

Balsamic vinegar and olive oil

4 pigeon breasts, skinned

Mixed salad leaves – e.g. beetroot, rocket
and chicory

1 shallot, peeled and finely diced

75 g (3 oz) toasted pine or walnuts

Seasoning

For the Dressing

2½ tablespoons sherry vinegar

100 ml (3½ fl oz) olive oil

3½ tablespoons walnut/hazelnut oil

Seasoning

Begin by making the dressing: whisk the oils and vinegar together and season.

Roast the beets by wrapping them in a parcel of tinfoil, loosely sealed together with the balsamic vinegar, olive oil and a generous amount of seasoning. Herbs such as marjoram as well as a few garlic cloves may also be added. The beets take ages to cook so allow plenty of time but once prepared in this way which accentuates their natural sweet earthiness, you will seldom cook them in any other way.

Season the pigeon breasts and heat a heavy-based frying pan with a slick of olive oil. When hot, add the pigeon and cook for approximately 3 minutes on one side and 2 minutes on the other, basting frequently and adding a nut of butter towards the end. Transfer to a warm place and leave, covered, to rest. Deglaze the pan with a little of the dressing and a splash of water, then add the rest of the dressing to heat through.

To serve, toss the salad leaves and shallot in the warm dressing, add the nuts and beetroot. Carve the pigeon into thin diagonal slices and arrange on top of the salad.

Tips from the Sink ~

• *Vary the vinegar for this dressing: try raspberry or even a splash of cassis.*

• *Crisply fried lardons also make a delicious addition.*

Thai Beef Salad

2 x 150 g (5 oz) sirloin steaks

Butter

1 x 2.5 cm (1 inch) piece of root ginger,
    peeled and thinly julienned

1 stem lemon grass, outer leaves removed
    and finely sliced

1–2 red chillies, seeded and finely diced

3 tablespoons fish sauce (Nam Pla)

Zest and juice of 3 limes

2 tablespoons soft brown sugar

1 red onion, peeled and thinly sliced in
    rings

Assorted washed salad leaves

Baby sweetcorn, sugar snap peas and bean
    sprouts, blanched

Tin water chestnuts, drained

Cherry tomatoes, halved

1 x cup mixed herbs: coriander, basil and
    mint, chopped

Cashew nuts

Seasoning

Season the steaks and smear one side of each with a little softened butter. Heat the griddle pan until very hot then pan fry for one minute on each side, so they remain rare. Remove and leave to cool then slice into thin diagonal strips.

In a large bowl, mix together the ginger, lemon grass, chillies, fish sauce, lime juice and zest, and sugar before tossing in the steak. Not everyone enjoys the taste of raw onion so, to remove the pungency, place the rings in a sieve and pour over a kettle of boiling water to blanche. Repeat the process – it removes that 'raw sting flavour'. When cool, add these to the above ingredients and mix in well.

Arrange the salad leaves on a large platter together with the baby corn, sugar snaps, bean sprouts, water chestnuts and cherry tomatoes. Add the beef mixture and finish by sprinkling over an abundance of the herbs followed by the cashew nuts.

Tip from the Sink ~

If you are making this for a large number of people, use a whole fillet of beef instead of the sirloin steaks.

Domestic God's Salad

This salad possesses more masculine power than feminine charm so – one for the men rather than the boys! Like kedgeree, it is good to eat at any time of the day or night.

300 g (12 oz) waxy potatoes
175 g (6 oz) black pudding
Olive oil
Wine vinegar – red or white
1 teaspoon wholegrain mustard

Token few lettuce leaves
8 slices Parma ham, cooked gammon,
　　grilled bacon or any other pork product
3 duck/bantam or hen's eggs
Seasoning

Begin by cooking the potatoes until just tender. Drain and when they are cool enough to handle, cut into slices about 5 mm (¼ inch thick). Remove the skin from the black pudding then cut into rounds about 1 cm (⅓ inch) thick. Heat 1 tablespoon olive oil in a frying pan and sauté the pudding on both sides until coloured and cooked through. Remove and set to one side then fry off the potatoes – adding a little more oil as necessary – until crisp and golden brown. Use also some crushed garlic if wished. Deglaze the pan with a little red or white wine vinegar then mix in the mustard and some more oil. Swirl around in the pan to combine.

Shove the leaves onto plates, pile on the potatoes, black pudding, bacon etc. then dress. Cook the eggs – poach, fry or softly boil (in which case peel) and top each portion with one egg per person, a twist of black pepper and pour over some dressing. Serve immediately with crusty bread.

Tip from the Sink ~

Chorizo sausage would also be good to include, so would sautéed duck livers, a tin of drained escargots warmed through with garlic butter or, for something altogether gutsier and more substantial, add a grilled pork or Barnsley chop.

Soups, Starters and Salads

Crispy Duck Salad with Watercress and Coriander

4 duck legs

2 star anise

2–3 fat cloves garlic, each one sliced in half

Chunk fresh root ginger, roughly chopped

2 tablespoons chopped coriander leaves
  (reserve stalks)

Vegetable oil for deep frying

4 handfuls watercress, washed and picked
  over, tough stalks removed

Handful sugar snaps, baby sweetcorn or
  bamboo shoots, cooked

2 tablespoons toasted sesame seeds

For the Dressing

3 tablespoons warm honey

4 tablespoons tomato ketchup

125 ml (4 fl oz) soy sauce (light or dark)

1 tablespoon sherry vinegar

½ teaspoon English mustard

3½ tablespoons sesame oil

125 ml (4 fl oz) vegetable oil

Put the duck legs, star anise, garlic and ginger into a pan and add the coriander stalks then cover with water. Bring to the boil, then turn the heat down and simmer gently for approx 45 minutes until the meat is tender. Drain and leave the duck to cool and then strip the meat from the bone and discard the skin. Tear into even sized pieces.

Mix the sauce ingredients together by warming the honey then adding the ketchup, soy sauce, sherry vinegar and mustard and finish by whisking in the oils.

Heat the vegetable oil in a deepish frying pan until sizzling then cook the meat off until crisp. Remove and mix in with the sauce so that each piece is well coated. Toss the duck into a bowl with the watercress leaves, cooked vegetables and the sesame seeds. Divide amongst four plates then sprinkle over the coriander leaves and serve.

Tip from the Sink ～

To warm the honey, stand the jar on the side of the Aga or in a basin of boiling hot water.

Salade Tiède of Griddled Scallops and Bacon with Hazelnut Beurre Blanc

Tiède means warm in French and it is a popular way in which to serve salads. Griddled scallops have to be one of my most favourite foods. They are simplicity itself to cook if you follow this method which takes no time at all. Resist, however, the temptation to poach them in liquid as they can very quickly become disappointingly chewy.

6 rashers back bacon	*For the Sauce*
100 g (4 oz) French beans, topped and tailed	1 shallot, peeled and finely diced
12 plump scallops, corals removed and reserved, membranes cleaned away	Large glass white wine
	Splash white wine vinegar
Olive oil	Bay leaf
Baby spinach leaves, washed	275 ml (½ pint) double cream
Seasoning	100–150 g (4–5 oz) cold butter, cubed
	Seasoning
	Hazelnut oil

Begin by making the sauce. Put the shallot and bay leaf into a saucepan, add the white wine and vinegar and set over the heat. Reduce the liquid until almost dry – i.e. one tablespoon remaining. Add the double cream and reduce slightly then whisk in the butter and season. Strain the sauce, return to the pan and add the hazelnut oil. Set aside until required.

Cook the bacon and roughly chop or crumble. Boil the beans over a fast heat until just cooked through, drain and set aside to keep warm. Steep the cleaned scallops in olive oil and sea salt. Heat a griddle or heavy-based frying pan until very hot. Arrange the spinach leaves on individual plates. Sear the scallops together with the corals briefly on both sides (approx 1 minute each side) until nicely browned and caramelised then divide amongst the plates along with the beans and bacon and pour over the warmed sauce.

Tip from the Sink ～

This salad is also excellent when made with cooked smoked haddock.

Roasted Blue Cheese Pears in a Rocket and Walnut Salad

A neat way of encompassing pudding, cheese and savoury courses!

50 g (2 oz) walnut pieces

300 g (11 oz) Gorgonzola or similar soft
  blue cheese

6 ripe pears, peeled and cored

Juice of ½ lemon

100 g (4 oz) rocket leaves

2 handfuls mixed salad leaves, torn

1 tablespoon white wine vinegar

1 tablespoon walnut oil

2 tablespoons extra virgin olive oil

Preheat the oven to 200°C/400°F/gas mark 6. Put the walnuts in a dry frying pan and roast in the oven or on top of the stove for about 8–10 minutes until they begin to release a strong nutty aroma and are lightly browned. Remove and set aside.

Put the cheese in a bowl and mash with a fork then season to taste. Toss the pear halves in the lemon juice then fill each cavity with some of the cheese mixture. Brush an ovenproof dish with olive oil and sit the filled pears, cut side uppermost, within. Bake in the oven for 20 minutes or so until the pears are lightly cooked and the cheese is bubbling.

Put the rocket and salad leaves plus the walnuts in a mixing bowl. In a separate bowl, whisk together the vinegar and the two oils and season to taste. Dress the salad and distribute between the plates. Top with the pear halves and serve immediately.

Roasted Butternut, Pine Nut, Mozzarella and Bacon Salad with Croutons

1 butternut, halved lengthways and seeded

Olive oil

5–6 rashers back bacon

2 buffalo mozzarella cheese, drained

3 slices white bread, crusts removed, slightly stale, cut into small cubes

Few lettuce leaves

Classic vinaigrette

75 g (3 oz) pine nuts, lightly toasted

Seasoning

Preheat the oven to 190°C/375°F/gas mark 5. Chop the butternut into chunks (no need to peel it) and heat some olive oil in a baking tray. Add the butternut and roast in the oven for approximately 20 minutes until nicely browned and soft. Remove, drain off on kitchen paper and set to one side.

Grill or fry the bacon until crisp then roughly chop. Tear the mozzarella cheeses up using fingers.

Add some more olive oil to a frying pan and sauté the bread until crisp on both sides.

To assemble, combine the butternut, bacon, cheese and bread with the lettuce leaves. Dress the salad with the vinaigrette, season then sprinkle over the pine nuts.

Summer's Day Salad

This looks wonderful on a plate with its pretty combination of colours and may be served either warm or cold, whichever is most convenient to the cook. For this dish, you need a fish that breaks into large flakes once cooked. I have used salmon here but sea trout, haddock or red mullet make good alternatives. The only other stipulation is that the broad beans must be double de-podded – those awful 'leather jackets' they wear have to go!

2 bulbs fennel, fronds reserved

1 large orange

4 middle cut salmon fillets

2 large handfuls cooked broad beans, outer
  shells removed

Handful black olives

Olive oil

2–3 heads of chicory, leaves separated

Seasoning

Preheat the oven to 180°C/350°F/gas mark 4. Trim both ends off the fennel and reserve the feathery fonds. Slice the heads thinly. Pare several strips of rind from the orange, set these to one side and squeeze the juice from the fruit.

Place the fennel, orange rind, juice and olive oil in an ovenproof dish and season. Bake in the oven until the fennel just begins to soften – you want it to retain a little bite – then remove from the heat.

Place the salmon fillets on an oiled baking sheet or tray, season and bake in the oven, skin side down, for approximately 10–12 minutes until just done then flake up, discarding the skin.

If the salad is to be served warm, either pour a kettle of boiling water over the beans in a sieve or put them in a bowl in the oven covered with cling-film to heat through. Arrange the chicory leaves on plates, followed by the fish, beans, olives and fennel. Pour over the cooking juices from the fennel as a dressing and season generously with black pepper. Decorate with the fennel fronds and serve.

Tip from the Sink ⌇

If you wish to accentuate the aniseed flavour, then try adding a splash of Pernod to the fennel whilst it is cooking.

Catherine's Salade Niçoise

Everyone needs a friend like Catherine Chichester. Warm and friendly — she is a natural cook and hostess as well as a passionate sourceress of the finest organic ingredients. Her capacious fridge and larder are always temptingly well stocked and I could happily spend a month locked away in either! This is her own up-market branding of a timeless classic.

Loin of tuna – sashimi or yellow fin quality, marinate the tuna for at least an hour beforehand.

For the Marinade
Either from a ready-made bottle or to include:
Terriyaki
Soy sauce
Sesame or ground nut oil
Grated ginger
Chopped garlic
Spoonful soft brown sugar
Lime or lemon juice

Salad leaves
New potatoes, peeled and cooked
Green beans cooked al dente
Eggs, lightly boiled and shelled

For the Dressing
4 tablespoons olive oil
1 tablespoon each white wine vinegar and lemon juice
1 clove garlic, crushed
1 teaspoon Dijon mustard
Roughly smashed stoned olives, e.g. tagliesca
Seasoning

Make up the dressing, season, and mix in the olives.

In a large bowl or flat dish, arrange the salad leaves, potatoes, beans and eggs. Remove the tuna from its marinade and sear in a hot dry pan until it forms a nice burnt crust on the outside and is still raw in the middle. If it looks like burning, simply spoon in a little of the marinade. Using a very sharp knife, thinly slice and lay over the other ingredients. Squirt with some lemon juice and add the dressing.

Tip from the Sink ⁓

Make up a large quantity of the olive dressing and keep the rest in a jar in the fridge for future use.

Flat Leaf Parsley and Shallot Salad

Rapidly assembled, this makes a happy bedfellow for grilled chicken or fish.

2 large bunches flat leaf parsley, stems
   discarded, well washed and dried
1 shallot, peeled and very finely chopped

Squirt lemon juice
Finest olive oil
Seasoning

Simply mix the parsley leaves with the shallot, add the lemon juice and olive oil, and season generously.

Tip from the Sink ∼

If you don't enjoy the strident flavour of raw shallots, simply tip them (once chopped) into a sieve and pour over a kettle of boiling water to soften their strength.

Easter Egg Salad

Country Channel TV is an independent broadcasting company. Together we made a programme on foraging in the springtime hedgerows and this salad featured amongst the recipes I offered. The green leaves used include ground elder – if only one could eat all that grows in the garden! – dandelion, torn wild garlic (also known as ramsons) and sorrel leaves bulked out, if necessary, with some ordinary lettuce. Use only those eggs with the finest orange free-range yolks.

4 free-range eggs, lightly boiled and peeled	Classic vinaigrette
6 bacon rashers, rind removed	Wild chives, finely scissored
Dandelion, ground elder, sorrel and wild garlic leaves	Primrose or cowslip flowers

Begin by boiling the eggs – 4½ minutes is ideal so that the yolks remain slightly runny in the centre. Peel and set aside. Fry the bacon rashers in a pan until crisp then drain on kitchen paper and cut into snippets, reserving the fat in the pan. Arrange the leaves on a large ashet or in a wide shallow bowl. Scatter over the bacon then halve the eggs and dot these around on top. Add the vinaigrette to the bacon fat and reheat until gently sizzling then pour over the salad to dress lightly and finish with the chives and flowers. Serve with warm crusty bread.

Kitchen Suppers in Kitten Heels

I LOVE EATING IN MY KITCHEN. It's the heart of the house, the hub of the engine and its all-pervading homely aura draws friends and guests, both human and canine! Perhaps this is to do with Aga which the dogs definitely regard as their own personal form of central heating. Whatever its magic potion, it's all things to all men. I live in it (well – virtually), I cook and entertain in it as well as holding many of my cooking demonstrations in it. With its well-scrubbed ancient pine table occupying pole position down the length of it, it's ideal for cosy gatherings. It means I need not miss out on all the chitchat and it bothers me not one jot if people congregate under my size five's as I potter around chopping, slicing and dicing. Furthermore, any offers of help at this juncture are always accepted with alacrity.

Kitchen suppers in kitten heels are not intended as a gastronomic fashion show but merely as a step-up from the microwave moment or fast food fix. They're all about something slick and snappy which looks and tastes good and is pretty much hassle free – ideal for informal and impromptu get-togethers.

There are but two simple tricks to remember when eating in the kitchen. First – if you have one – turn on the extractor fan before you commence cooking and if, like me, you do not, then light a scented candle to absorb those smells! Second, to prevent the worktop surfaces looking like a bombsite, shove any pots and pans you may not have time to wash up out of sight or pile them neatly in a corner and throw a tea towel (or two) over the lot. Nothing is worse than staring at a pile of dirty dishes though, with careful recycling, you will be amazed how few pans are really needed. Then dim the lights!

Fish

Many people are nervous about cooking fish and limit their skills in this direction to a fairly run-of-the-mill fish pie. Piscatorial delights are, however, one of the easiest and quickest ingredients to handle and, the fresher the fish, the less one needs to do to it. Think of plain grilled Dover sole, barbecued mackerel straight from the sea or a piece of poached turbot with hollandaise sauce – all wondrous fishy treats.

When buying fish, look for the following key pointers. The stiffer the better; the shinier and more gleaming the skin; the brighter and more prominent the eye and the redder the gills – all are important considerations when making your selection. Smell, too, is critical and really fresh fish does not possess any – other than a faint salty whiff of the sea. Be prepared always to seek advice from your fishmonger – he will know what is best on the day – and to buy by eye, rejecting anything that looks limp, tired or sub-standard. It's obvious, also, to purchase the fish that is sitting on a bed of crushed ice on the slab to keep it cool.

Baked Fish with Herbs and Lemons

This is a great way of cooking whole, gutted fish and the end result is improved further by the mouth-watering aroma which escapes when you open up the parcel before serving. The cooking juices contained within are all that is needed in the way of a sauce. Use at least four of the selection of herbs listed below. Whether you are feeding two people with say, a smallish sea bass, or a greater number with a sea trout or large salmon this is pure, clean unadulterated food at its best – unbeatable!

2 whole sea bass – around 750 g (1¾ lb) each or 1 sea trout – around 1½ kg (3 lbs) – cleaned and gutted	Few bay leaves
	2–3 lemon grass stems, slit in half lengthways
2 tablespoons olive oil	1 large lemon, sliced
Handful rosemary, tarragon, basil, sage, thyme sprigs	Seasoning

Preheat the oven to 180°C/350°F/gas mark 4. Scale the fish (or ask your fishmonger to do this for you) by scraping the blade of a sharp knife over the skin surface, and discarding all the scales which come away then, with the tip of the knife, score the skin on both sides with several slashes. Wash the inside of the fish well and pat dry with kitchen paper.

Rub the fish all over with seasoning and olive oil. Lay a large sheet of tin foil in a baking sheet and scatter with the herbs and lemon grass, and slip one or two slices of lemon inside the cavity of the fish and dot the remainder around. Drizzle over a little more olive oil and cover loosely with a second sheet of foil and crimp the edges firmly to seal. The foil should form a roomy tent around the fish, allowing space for the steam to actually cook the fish. Place in the oven and bake for approximately 25 minutes (larger fish will take a little longer) until the fish is only just cooked. Remove from the heat and leave to rest, still wrapped, for 10 minutes before serving. Simply bring to the table, unwrap, savour the heavenly smell and spoon the cooking juices over the fish as you serve it.

Fish in a Salt Crust

This is another wonderfully easy, un-mucked around way of serving a whole fish. Once again, all the goodness is captured within and the flavour is divine so let this sing out on its own. Presented at the table still in its salt crust, it evokes that touch of culinary drama without causing the cook undue stress!

1 whole fish to serve 4 – cleaned and gutted	2 egg whites
2 x 450 g (1 lb) packets sea salt	Fistful of herbs

Preheat the oven to 180°C/350°F/gas mark 4. Scale the fish by scraping the skin all over with a sharp knife and then wipe clean. In a bowl, whisk two egg whites until firm then mix in the salt. Stuff the cavity of the fish with as many herbs as possible (this will prevent the salt from invading it too much). Lay the fish on a non-stick baking tray and cover all with a blanket of salt mixture. If there is not quite enough due to the fish being rather large, then don't worry about the tail. Slide into the oven and cook for around 25–30 minutes until the salt crust is just beginning to colour then remove from the heat and leave to stand for approximately 10 minutes.

To serve, simply break the crust, discard and peel off the skin. Wedges of lemon and perhaps some buttery new potatoes are the only necessary accompaniments.

Plain Simple Fishcakes

Nothing beats a home-made fishcake and I like to keep mine really simple with as few ingredients as possible. The secret is a 50:50 ratio of potato to fish. I make these when I have some leftover poached salmon or sea trout. They are also great with haddock. Remember too that, like kedgeree, fishcakes are good to eat at any time of the day – or night!

450 g (1 lb) cooked fish, roughly flaked and boned

1 tablespoon cooking juices from the fish

450 g (1 lb) mashed potato – use a floury variety such as Maris Piper

2 large tablespoons chopped flat leaf parsley

Groundnut oil

Plain flour

2 eggs, whisked

Breadcrumbs

Seasoning

Do not be tempted to start adding butter, milk or cream to the seasoned potatoes – you want to keep them dry. If, however, you have some cooking juices left over from the fish, then mash in a tablespoon of these, followed by the parsley. Fold in the fish by hand – too much vigorous beating will break up the pieces too much and reduce everything to a mush. Shape into rounds – roughly the size of the palm of your hand – dip in a dish of flour, followed by the egg mixture then coat with the breadcrumbs.

To cook, simply heat some groundnut or sunflower oil in a large shallow frying pan so that it comes about a third of the way up its sides and, when hot, sauté the fishcakes in batches on both sides until golden brown and crisp. Stand on kitchen paper to blot then serve with either hollandaise or tartare sauce.

Tip from the Sink ∽

Replace the parsley with coriander and offer with a sweet chilli dipping sauce.

Steamed Fillets of Fish

It was Christian Germain who first introduced me to cooking both fish and poultry with cling-film. In his kitchens they had an enormous steel machine, like some monstrous water tank on legs with a rolling lid. It was filled with simmering water and into it went all manner of ingredients to be cooked 'en vapeur'. I had never seen anything like this before and thought it the height of culinary sophistication. My own translation of such equipment is somewhat more basic and consists of a rather humbler saucepan on top of the stove but the end result is still very good! Some people are horrified by the thought of cooking with cling-film but don't be. All makes today are 'cook friendly' and hence safe to use.

4 x 175 g (6 oz) fillets of fish – e.g. haddock, sea or black bream, sea bass – with skin on, any small bones removed with tweezers	Handful tarragon, dill or basil leaves Olive oil Seasoning

Using the tip of a sharp knife, score the skin of each fillet at 1 cm (½ inch) intervals, season and lay each one, skin side down, on a large piece of cling-film (large enough to wrap each one into an individual secure parcel). Season the flesh side of each fillet, anoint with a little olive oil and then add a few herbs. Wrap up each fillet tightly, twisting the ends of the cling-film and tying each one in a secure knot. Make sure the fillets of fish remain flat.

Bring a large saucepan of water to the boil then reduce to a simmer – just so the odd bubble breaks the surface. Slide in the fish parcels and poach gently for approximately 10 minutes until the fish is opaque. Unwrap one, pour off any liquid which may have seeped in and check it is cooked though in the centre. If not rewrap and poach for a further couple of minutes.

To serve, remove the cling-film and place the fish, skin side uppermost, on a bed of samphire if you can find it. Alternatively, go for summer vegetables such as peas, broad beans and baby carrots. Drizzle over a little more olive oil, add some sea salt and decorate with a couple of herb sprigs or leaves.

Salmon with Red Cabbage and Red Wine Sauce

Red cabbage is, of course, at its zenith during the winter months. Although more usually associated with hearty casseroles, stews and game it also makes a great partner to salmon. I often serve this dish for supper over the Christmas period when it makes a scintillating change from the turkey, ham and goose routine.

1 red cabbage – at least 1 kg (2 lbs)

2 red onions, peeled and thinly sliced

2 large cooking apples, peeled, quartered and cored

Pinch ground cloves

Rasping nutmeg

Juice and zest of an orange

Cranberries

Handful plump sultanas

2 tablespoons red wine vinegar

Large glass of red wine

Soft brown sugar

25 g (1 oz) butter

Seasoning

4 middle cut fillets of salmon, skinned

Lemon juice

Seasoning

For the Sauce

300 ml (½ pint) chicken stock

2 glasses red wine

Splash of port or cassis

Squeeze lemon juice

Redcurrant jelly or brown sugar if needed

Seasoning

Preheat the oven to approximately 140°C/275°F/gas mark 1. Begin by cooking the cabbage. Discard the outer tough leaves of the cabbage, quarter it, remove the hard white core then shred finely. Pile some into a large casserole which has a lid, add some onions, slices of apple, a little of the spices, zest, cranberries, sultanas and seasoning and repeat this layering process until everything is in then add the wine vinegar, red wine, orange juice, sugar and butter. Cover and cook in the oven very slowly for at least 3 hours, remembering to give everything an occasional stir and add a little more liquid if you think it may need some.

To make the sauce, reduce the chicken stock by at least half, then add the red wine and reduce again until quite syrupy. Add the port or cassis, seasoning and a squirt of lemon juice and leave on the heat. Taste and adjust as necessary. If it needs a little sweetening, then add a blob of redcurrant jelly or a pinch of brown sugar.

Preheat the oven to 190°C.

Place the salmon fillets on a baking sheet, season and add a squeeze of lemon juice to each one. Cook in the oven for approximately 12 minutes until just done.

To serve, arrange the red cabbage on a large plate, add the fish and pour over some of the sauce then hand round the rest in a jug.

Tip from the Sink ∼

When reducing liquids, do so in a saucepan with a pale coloured, rather than dark, interior. It makes it so much easier to judge by how little or much the ingredients have evaporated.

Monte Carlo Fish Pie

So called because of the speed with which this can be made. Forget the standard white sauce and the sautéing of onions etc. Skip, also, the unnecessary process of poaching the fish beforehand. This can be rustled up in a matter of minutes and is a runaway favourite.

450 g (1 lb) fillet smoked (undyed) haddock, skinned and boned or smaller fillets of white fish, e.g. cod, haddock etc.

4 hard-boiled eggs

1 x 450 g (1 lb) tub crème fraîche

150 g (5 oz) grated mature cheddar or Parmesan cheese – or a mixture

2–3 tomatoes, thinly sliced

Handful chopped parsley leaves – optional

Seasoning

Rasping of nutmeg

Preheat the oven to 180°C/350°F/gas mark 4. Cut the fish into bite-sized pieces. Hard boil the eggs then stand in cold water to cool before peeling and halving. Empty the crème fraîche into a saucepan and bring gently to the boil then add the cheese and stir to melt. Allow to bubble for a few minutes as this will also help thicken the mixture. Season together with the nutmeg and mix in the parsley.

To assemble, place the fish in an ovenproof dish and dot around the eggs then pour over the sauce. Arrange the tomato slices on top and bake in the oven until browned and bubbling (approximately 20 minutes) by which time the fish will be cooked through.

Tip from the Sink ⁓

Vary this pie by including some salmon and a handful of prawns. Top it with creamy mashed potato.

Salmon with Pernod Sauce

4 x thick fillets salmon (preferably wild),
   skinned, any pinbones removed
Olive oil

For the Sauce
150 ml (5 fl oz) light chicken stock

4–5 tablespoons crème fraîche or double
   cream
Pernod to taste
1 tablespoon chopped tarragon leaves
Squeeze lemon juice
Seasoning

Reduce the stock down to a couple of tablespoons by which time it will be syrupy in consistency. Whisk in the cream and Pernod plus the seasoning then set aside.

To cook the fish, rub both sides of the fillets with olive oil and season. Heat a heavy-based non-stick frying pan until hot, then add the salmon, skin side down, and cook for approximately 7–8 minutes or until it is done. Alternatively, bake in the oven if the extractor fan is not up to whisking away that awful fishy odour which so quickly pervades not only the kitchen but the entire house!

To finish the sauce, return to the heat and warm through before adding the tarragon at the last minute and a squeeze of lemon juice. Serve with some roasted fennel.

Tip from the Sink ∼

Not everyone is a fan of Pernod. Noilly Prat makes a very good substitute and there is always a bottle in my drinks cupboard. After all, there is little wrong with a well-made Vodka Martini especially when the Noilly is passed over its surface! Since it is a type of fortified wine, the bottle doesn't need to be kept in the fridge once opened.

Seared Scallops with Jerusalem Artichoke Purée

This has to rank amongst my Top Ten Dishes. It features on the menu at Le Caprice and, though my own version here may be somewhat less fine-tuned, it is still sublimely good. The ambrosial earthiness of this vegetable makes a peerless partner to the sweetness of these molluscs.

16–20 plump fresh scallops

450g–750 g (1–1½ lbs) Jerusalem
    artichokes, cleaned and peeled

Juice of half a lemon

2–3 tablespoons crème fraîche

Rasping of nutmeg

Olive oil

100 g (4 oz) butter

1 crushed garlic clove

2 tablespoons flat leaf parsley,
    chopped

Sea salt

Clean the scallops by removing the corals (reserve these) and removing the membrane and any fibrous parts. Steep in a little olive oil and scatter over some sea salt.

Next, place the artichokes in a pan of boiling, salted water which has been acidulated with the juice of half a lemon to prevent discolouration and cook for approximately 20 minutes until perfectly tender. Drain thoroughly and return to the heat, cover with a tea towel to absorb any extra liquid, for a few minutes shaking the pan vigorously. Purée until smooth in a liquidiser, add the crème fraîche and the nutmeg. Keep warm.

Melt a little of the butter in a pan, add the garlic and cook without letting it catch, add the rest of the butter and swirl around until it is hot but not burning. Toss in the parsley. Heat a dry, heavy-based griddle pan until very hot, then quickly sear the scallops on both sides until nicely browned and caramelised. This won't take long – just a minute or so on each side. To serve, place a puddle of purée on each (warmed) plate or in a shallow bowl, dot over the scallops and pour around the garlic butter.

Tip from the Sink ~

Artichoke soup, topped with seared scallops, is another great way of enjoying this duo of ingredients.

Kitchen Suppers in Kitten Heels

Tagliatelle of Mussels in Gerwurztraminer

Mussels in white wine and even cider are standard fare but try them with this Alsatian wine – there will be plenty left in the bottle for a glass or two! The almost iodine-like flavour of this shellfish is a winning combination with the purity of this particular grape variety.

1 kg (2¼ lbs) mussels
300 ml (½ pint) Gerwurztraminer wine
Large shallot, peeled and finely chopped
4 tablespoons crème fraîche
Zest of a lemon

Flat leaf parsley, chopped
Seasoning

400 g (14 oz) fresh tagliatelle

Begin by putting the mussels in a basin or bucket of cold water and scrubbing them well to clean. Pull away the beards and discard any shells which are open and which do not close when tapped. Heat half the wine in a large pan, then add the mussels and cover with a lid. Steam for 3–4 minutes until they have just opened then remove from the heat and, using a slotted spoon, transfer to a dish. Quickly pass the cooking liquid through a fine sieve (this will get rid of any particles of grit etc.) and return to the pan then add the rest of the wine together with the shallot and reduce by half. Stir in the crème fraîche, lemon zest and season. Shell the mussels leaving a few intact for decoration, and keep warm.

Cook the pasta in the usual way, in plenty of boiling salted water, drain and return to the pan together with the sauce and mussels and mix well. Transfer to a warmed serving dish, scatter on the parsley and top with the mussels in their shells.

Tip from the Sink ～

If you do not possess a fine sieve, simply line the inside of an ordinary one with either a coffee filter, a piece of muslin or kitchen paper.

Poultry

A plump, organically raised, free-range, corn-fed chicken is what good food is all about. With its fine pedigree, it is a far cry from those intensively reared, plastic-wrapped birds which flood supermarket shelves. Such inferior species yield flavourless flesh filled with water and only ever disappoint. A proper chicken, on the other hand, which in an ideal world has been hung and comes complete with giblets and liver (the former is good for the stockpot or gravy whilst the latter can be turned into pâté) epitomises the best of honest, unpretentious British comfort food. Roasted with herbs, lemon and olive oil, its thick skin (factory farmed birds always have tell-tale thin skins which tear easily) cooked to a crisp, golden crackle; it is always a source of joy. And the same goes for the Christmas turkey.

A chicken is a bird of many guises and may be transformed into literally hundreds of mouth-watering culinary delights since it adapts well to all types of different ingredients as well as to different means of cooking – both gleaned from all over the world. Whether poached, grilled, griddled or casseroled – from robust bourgeois coq au vin style dishes; hot, pungent curries to enveloping delicate, willow-the-wisp creamy tarragon based sauces – is delightfully and endlessly versatile.

Griddled Lemon and Herb Chicken Escalopes

The pure, zesty flavour of the lemon alongside the fresh tasting herbs makes this a great summer dish which is quick and easy to prepare.

4 chicken fillets, skinned

3–4 tablespoons mixed fresh herbs, e.g.
thyme leaves, marjoram, mint, parsley,
tarragon, chives etc

Juice and zest of 2 lemons

Seasoning

Olive oil

Lay the chicken fillets, one at a time, in a sturdy polythene bag and beat out evenly to flatten to make large thin escalopes. Place them in a large shallow dish and marinate with the herbs, lemon, olive oil and seasoning. Dry heat a griddle or ridged pan (otherwise a non-stick frying pan will do perfectly well) until very hot and sear the chicken pieces until nicely charred on both sides. They won't take that long as they are less thick than ordinary chicken breasts (probably about 2 minutes per side). Set to one side and serve, very simply, with lemon wedges.

Tip from the Sink ~

Wedged inside a fresh baguette, split lengthways, this makes a sublimely good hot sarni as the juices seep into the bread.

Poulet de Licques Roti and Farci

This somewhat intimidating title should not put you off. In fact, this recipe comes from M. Christian Germain of Chateau de Montreuil fame. Licques is the name of a local nearby village from which this fowl takes its name. The pocket between the skin and flesh of the bird is filled with a delicious cream cheese and herb stuffing whose flavours impart themselves wonderfully well throughout the cooking and help prevent the meat from drying out. When numbers expand, I like to roast two chickens in this way (allowing slightly longer cooking time) and bring them to the table on a large board with a couple of large knives and forks leaving friends to hack away for themselves!

1½ kg (3–3½ lbs) free-range chicken	Lemon juice
1 x 200 g (7 oz) tub full fat soft cheese	Seasoning
100 g (4 oz) butter, softened	Olive oil
1 peeled shallot, finely diced	Large nut of butter
1 tablespoon snipped herbs such as parsley,	Unskinned onion, roughly chopped
tarragon and chives	Thyme, rosemary and bay leaves

Preheat the oven to approximately 190°C/375°F/gas mark 5. In a bowl, mix the cream cheese and butter together then add the shallot, herbs, lemon juice and seasoning.

Using fingers, separate the skin from the flesh of the bird by means of gentle oscillation, being careful not to tear the skin. Pack the mixture between the two, squeezing down over the legs of the bird and pat with your hands to re-shape!

Melt some olive oil and butter in a roasting tin, throw in the onion and toss around. When hot add the bird and tuck the herbs around. Cook for approximately 55 minutes, basting with the juices regularly. (This may seem rather an effort but it does make all the difference to the end result!). Pierce the thigh with a skewer to check if cooked and when it is done, remove from the oven, cover with tin foil and rest in a warm place. Meanwhile, discard the herbs from the pan then add a splash of water (or white wine) to the pan and reduce the liquid to make a very simple jus. The onion is now deliciously soft and unctuously sweet. Either serve as it is in chunks or whip off the skin and mash the flesh into the jus.

Creamy mashed potato and some purple sprouting are perfect partners to this.

Tips from the Sink ∿

- *When cooking poultry, meat and game always bring it to room temperature before putting it into the oven.*

- *Once done, remove from the heat, cover with a double layer of tin foil and a few tea towels (or even an old, clean, towel) and leave to rest for the same length of time as it spent in the oven. This way the muscles relax, the meat is easier to carve and has time to tenderise.*

Fred's Thai Chick

I christened this dish after Fred Barker, one of my most regular and popular Dishes with Dashers pupils. Fred is fascinated by food, its alchemy and chemistry and has a delightfully acquisitive mind – which keeps me up to the mark! He recently requested something Thai orientated ... so I thought a 'feathered' chick the best to offer.

The great glory about this is that, once the chopping and dicing are done, it takes only 10 minutes to cook and since only either a wok or frying pan is used (plus a saucepan for the noodles) the washing up is pretty minimal. Try substituting raw, shelled tiger prawns for a fishy alternative. You can add oomph by increasing the amounts of chilli and garlic if wished.

4 chicken breasts, skinned and cut into thin diagonal strips
1 tablespoon fish sauce – NamPla
1 tablespoon light soy sauce
400 g (14 oz) tin coconut milk
1 tablespoon light brown sugar
1 clove garlic, crushed
1 tablespoon peeled and grated root ginger
½ red chilli, halved lengthways, seeded and minutely chopped

½ bunch spring onions, white part only, finely chopped
175 g (6 oz) medium dried egg or rice noodles
Zest and juice of a lime
100 g (4 oz) tender baby spinach leaves, washed and dried
Handful coriander leaves, roughly chopped

In a wok, or a heavy-based or cast iron frying pan, heat up the fish and soy sauces together with the coconut milk. Stir in the sugar, then toss in the garlic, ginger, chilli and spring onions and cook to soften.

Meanwhile, in a separate pan boil the noodles in unsalted water (the fish sauce is very salty), drain when done and keep warm.

Add the lime zest and juice to the chicken pan and taste, adjusting flavours as necessary. You may wish to add more sugar/soy sauce or lime juice. Put the strips of chicken into the pan and let the heat just cook them through, turning them once – this takes only a few minutes. Finally, stir in the spinach leaves so they just wilt.

To serve, tip the noodles onto the base of a warmed meat or similar large plate, preferably one with a lip, and spoon over the contents of the wok/frying pan and to finish, scatter over the coriander leaves. Serve with wedges of lime.

Tip from the Sink ~

Limes are notoriously ungenerous in terms of the amount of juice they yield. To extract more, try heating them in the microwave for 10 seconds or place them on a work surface and, using the palm of your hand, roll the fruit around to soften, thereby encouraging better results when squeezed. Alternatively, finger and pinch them all relentlessly when purchasing to select only the softest, which are invariably the juiciest.

Stuffed Quail with Moorish Sauce

4 oven-ready quail
50 g (2 oz) butter
Olive oil
Ladle of wine or stock
Seasoning

For the Sauce
2 tablespoons soft brown sugar

Glass white wine
4 tablespoons jellied chicken stock
75 g (3 oz) sultanas, soaked in
    boiling water then drained
Grated zest of 2 lemons
Few shakes aged balsamic vinegar
Seasoning

Preheat the oven to 180°C/350°F/gas mark 4. Season the birds and heat the butter and oil in a pan on top of the stove. When sizzling, quickly brown the quail, breast side down until just nicely coloured. Add the wine/stock to the pan and transfer to the oven. Roast for approximately 15–18 minutes, basting once or twice if you remember, then remove and keep warm.

For the sauce put the sugar and wine into a small pan and bring gently to the boil, stirring carefully so the sugar dissolves. Add the sultanas, lemon zest and stock and simmer to reduce so that it becomes almost syrupy. Add the balsamic vinegar and season to taste.

Serve the quail on a bed of couscous containing toasted pine nuts, flat leaf parsley and some lemon zest or perhaps some cooked wild rice with leeks or mushrooms – or use as a stuffing to go inside the birds.

Tip from the Sink ～

The sauce is also very good served cold with say, poached chicken – in which case whisk in 100 ml (4 fl oz) olive oil. It goes well, too, with guinea fowl, glazed ham, slow roasted belly of pork and, when in season, pheasant.

Quail with Summer Tomato and Tarragon Vinaigrette

Redolent of summer, this recipe breathes its own rays of sunshine and is great for feeding either small or larger numbers of people. The original inspiration for this vinaigrette-style dressing came from Christian Germain who made a tomato-ey type dressing for warm chicken. It contains that ubiquitous store cupboard essential – tomato ketchup – which makes it very user-friendly. I've tweaked it here and there to come up with the following. It is great too with veal, tomato summer pudding or, indeed, a plain tomato and avocado salad. Or you could use it as a dressing for cold poached fish such as salmon. It will keep for up to a week in the fridge but, any longer, and it begins to lose its freshness. Try replacing the tarragon with either marjoram or basil – either works equally well.

6 quail

For the Sauce
4 tablespoons olive oil
Splash red wine vinegar
Pinch sugar
1 tablespoon chopped tarragon leaves
2 tablespoons tomato ketchup
Squirt of lemon juice

1 tablespoon warmed chicken stock
   (optional)
Worcester sauce – to taste
Shake of Tabasco sauce
2 vine or plum tomatoes, peeled, seeded
   and cored
Seasoning

Finely dice the tomatoes and set aside. In a large bowl, mix together the oil, red wine vinegar and then add the other ingredients including the stock if you are using it. Though not essential, it just lends a little more gravitas and oomph! Check for flavour then stir in the tomatoes. Leave to stand for an hour or so to allow flavours to develop.

Roast the birds in the usual way and leave to rest. I usually serve them whilst still just warm and pour on the sauce.

Game

For real sporting gourmets, pride of place belongs to the first grouse of the season. A keenly anticipated treat – it is a timely reminder in itself that autumn and another larder of goodies is only around the corner. The annual race of transporting these birds from the moors to the Capital's most fashionable restaurants in a matter of hours is an institution in its own right with as much over-rated hype and excitement surrounding it as the yearly Beaujolais Nouveau run. I mean, who can't wait a few days?

The subject of how long game should be hung for is a debatable topic – though, practically speaking, young birds should need only a few days to tenderise and sweeten the meat. Thereafter, it really depends on how 'high' the individual likes his game to be though I am happy to leave those birds which are literally 'walking' to the real masochists!

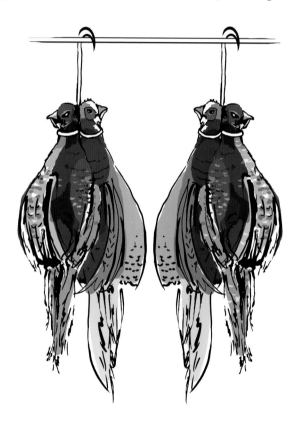

Roast Grouse with Red Wine Gravy

Go for broke here and serve grouse with its traditional accompaniments: breadcrumbs, watercress, game chips, lashings of bread sauce and a good rich gravy. Don't be afraid to pick the bird from the plate in your fingers and chew the flavoursome meat nestling around its carcase

1 young bird per person, plucked and drawn
50 g (2 oz) soft butter
4 bacon rashers
4 slices white bread
Juniper berries
Red wine
1 teaspoon Bovril

150 ml (¼ pint) chicken or game stock
1 teaspoon redcurrant jelly
Seasoning

Garnishes might include
Toasted breadcrumbs, Game chips,
Bread sauce, Watercress

Preheat the oven to 190°C/375°F/gas mark 5. Truss the birds in the usual way, season and smear all over with the butter. Add an extra nut of butter to the cavity of each grouse, plus a few juniper berries. Place the birds on a slice of well buttered bread – if wished, the livers may be mashed, seasoned and sautéed in butter for a few minutes then spread onto the croûtes. Place the grouse in a roasting tin, lay a bacon rasher over each one, add a splash of wine to the pan and roast in the oven for approximately 18 minutes, basting from time to time, then cover and rest in the usual way. If, for some reason, you are not planning to allow the birds to 'sit' after cooking, then you may wish to increase the actual time in the oven slightly.

For the gravy, deglaze the roasting tin with a little stock and boil hard to reduce before adding a glass of red wine, the Bovril and redcurrant jelly or a pinch of brown sugar and season to taste.

Tip from the Sink ～

Cold roasted grouse makes excellent picnic fare. Carve into thin slices and put inside floury white baps with jelly, such as rowan and apple.

Roast Partridge with Leek, Orange and Cardamon Sauce

This is a heavenly sauce to serve with partridge being neither too rich nor overpowering.

1 bird per person, preferably grey-legged
Butter, softened
4 rashers unsmoked bacon
Sprigs rosemary
Seasoning

For the Sauce
1 leek, white part only finely, sliced
50 g (2 oz) butter

300 ml (½ pint) chicken or game stock
Large glass white wine
Zest and juice of 1e large orange
Pinch or two of cardamon powder
Seasoning
Tot of brandy – to taste

Preheat the oven to 190°C/375°F/gas mark 5. Truss the birds, season and spread with a little butter then cover with the bacon. Tuck the rosemary into the cavity of each one and roast in the oven for around 18–20 minutes. Remove, cover and leave to rest. If the bacon still looks a bit pink, remove it and return it to the oven to crisp up.

For the sauce, sweat the leeks in the butter, covering the pan with a liquid to prevent them from burning, until soft. Next, add both the stock and the wine and reduce briskly by half. Pour in the orange juice, zest and brandy plus the cardamon and reduce again until quite syrupy. (For extra gloss, whisk in a few cubes of cold butter.) Check seasoning. Serve with Savoy cabbage or roasted root vegetables.

Tips from the Sink ～

- *The sauce can be prepared well in advance and reheated – making this an easy dish to serve for supper and dinner parties.*

- *Often you will find that one bird will be sufficient for two girls to share. Keep the carcases afterwards for the stockpot!*

Pheasant in Orange with Gin

The best pheasants to eat plainly roasted are wild, whose flesh is League Division One when compared to that of reared birds which are usually best when casseroled though, if I am being honest, my heart often sinks when I see the lid being whipped off a Le Creuset dish to reveal yet another old bird (usually peppered with shot) swimming around in a sea of watery stock – aka coloured water – and a few desultory carrots bobbing around. One glance at this tells you all you need to know – and would prefer not to! It is for this reason that I like to use my terracotta brick. Soak both parts in cold water for two hours beforehand then sit the bird inside, adding water and white wine plus carrots, celery stalks, peppercorns, onions, a few wands of trimmed leeks and a bouquet garni and simply poach. If, how-ever, you do not own this particular bit of equipment, then try this recipe instead which is remarkably good.

100 g (4 oz) butter, softened	1 tablespoon plain flour
2 birds	1 tablespoon redcurrant or rowan jelly
12 juniper berries, crushed	2 tablespoons orange juice
4 rashers streaky bacon, rinds removed	2 tablespoons gin
600 ml (1 pint) stock or cider, or half and half	Seasoning

Heat the oven to 190°C/375°F/gas mark 5. Put a quarter of the butter into the cavity of each bird and rub the remainder over their skins then season well. Place in a large casserole together with the juniper berries. Arrange the bacon rashers over the breasts of the birds and pour on half the stock/cider liquid, cover and cook for 45–55 minutes, basting several times, until tender and cooked through. To test if done, put the point of a knife or a skewer into the leg and see if the juices run clear.

Remove the pheasants and bouquet garni from the liquid and skim this to remove any fat, then stir in the flour. Beat until lump-free before whisking in the rest of the liquid, the redcurrant jelly, orange juice and gin. Taste for seasoning.

Carve the birds and return the pieces to the casserole, heating through gently to serve alongside some puréed sweet potato and carrots to which a little orange zest has been added.

Pheasant Breasts with Porcini Mushroom and White Truffle Sauce

This sauce packs a proper punch. Its appeal lies not only in its depth of flavour but also in the speed with which it can be concocted.

6 pheasant breasts, skinned

2 small eggs, beaten

3 tablespoons double cream or crème fraîche

Fresh thyme or sage leaves, finely chopped

Seasoning

Lemon zest (optional)

For the Sauce

300 ml (½ pint) jellied chicken stock

1 tablespoon Porcini Mushroom & White Truffle Sauce (available in supermarkets)

Dash of Madeira (or sherry) to taste

Seasoning

Squeeze of lemon juice

Sautéed sliced mushrooms (optional)

Begin by blending two of the pheasant breasts in the processor until minced then mix in the eggs, cream, herbs and seasoning. A little grated lemon zest may be added if wished. Open out the remaining pheasant breasts and put each one in a plastic bag and beat out slightly. Spread some of the stuffing over the surface of each one, roll up lengthways and wrap individually in cling-film. Bring a pan of water to the boil then poach the parcels in simmering water for approximately 10 minutes making sure you push them down under the water regularly with a wooden spoon. Remove and leave to rest in a warm place whilst making the sauce.

Reduce the chicken stock in a pan by two-thirds until syrupy then add the truffle sauce. Whisk in well then add the Madeira and seasoning. Taste to check the flavour is strong enough. Season, add a squeeze of lemon juice and toss in the mushrooms (if using) to heat through.

To serve, carve the pheasant into slices and sit on a bed of braised Savoy cabbage.

Pigeon with Pomegranate Dressing

Pigeon has no close season. It associates very well with fruits in general and especially pomegranates – prevalent in winter months. The availability of pre-prepared pomegranate seeds has revolutionised dishes such as this one in terms of swift execution. No more fiddling around extracting the flesh from the pithy white membranes!

8 pigeon breasts, cleaned
Olive oil
Butter
Seasoning

For the Dressing
1 pink grapefruit
Small packet fresh pomegranate
    seeds (available in supermarkets)

3 tablespoons cranberry juice
3 tablespoons freshly squeezed
    orange juice
6 tablespoons vinaigrette
2 tablespoons walnut oil

Begin by making the dressing. Cut the peel and pith from the grapefruit, catching the juices. Ease out the segments and set to one side. Blitz two-thirds of the pomegranate seeds with the cranberry, orange and grapefruit juices then sieve into a saucepan, pressing through as much as possible using the back of a spoon. Boil the juices and reduce by half until slightly syrupy, then whisk in the vinaigrette and walnut oil. Add the remaining pomegranate seeds, together with the grapefruit segments and check seasoning.

Season the pigeon breasts. Heat the olive oil and butter in a heavy-based frying pan and sauté the breasts for approximately 3 minutes on one side then turn over and cook the other side for 1½ minutes. Ideally, they should still be pink in the centre. Cover and leave to rest in a warm place.

To serve, slice the pigeon breasts diagonally and serve with wilted spinach and sautéed potatoes.

Oriental Duck

Diana Jary, who cooked at Gerrard & National where I worked for fourteen very happy years, gave me this universally popular recipe. In those days, City lunches were considered an important part of the working day and our famous Discount House enjoyed a well-earned reputation within the Square Mile for being not only one of the finest dining houses but also for possessing a fantastically classy cellar of wines. I was lucky enough to share the spoils from both!

It is best, if possible, to start this the day before you want to eat it.

3 large magret du canard, fat scored

For the Marinade
300 ml (½ pint) soy sauce – light or dark or a mixture
1 teaspoon Dijon mustard
2 tablespoons runny honey
Large bunch coriander, leaves and stalks separated
Knob of fresh ginger, peeled and grated
Clove of garlic, crushed

For the Sauce
300 ml (½ pint) chicken stock
1 teaspoon ground star anise or Five-Spice powder
1 teaspoon cornflour, slaked in a little chicken stock

Egg noodles
Sugar snap peas
250 g (8 oz) sliced mushrooms, sautéed in sesame oil

Mix together the marinade ingredients, using only the coriander stalks and keeping the leaves for the garnish, and put in a shallow dish together with the duck breasts. Cover and leave in a cold place for 12–24 hours.

For the sauce, strain the marinade into a saucepan and pour in the chicken stock, reserving 2 tablespoons to be blended with the cornflour. Add the star anise/Five-Spice powder, then stir in the cornflour and bring to the boil and reduce down until it reaches the required consistency. Check seasoning and set aside.

Preheat the grill until very hot and place the duck on a rack. Grill for approximately 12–14 minutes (depending upon how pink you like the meat) then cover and rest in a warm place.

Cook the noodles in the usual way tossing in the sugar snap peas just before the end. Drain and add the mushrooms then spoon out onto a large warmed platter and diagonally slice the duck breasts and arrange on top. Pour over the sauce and scatter with chopped coriander leaves.

Tip from the Sink ～

Large duck magrets, available from your butcher, are far superior to supermarket varieties. Three of these will serve four people comfortably

Sweet and Sour Duck Legs

4–6 duck legs

4 tablespoons runny honey

1 teaspoon Five-Spice powder

4 garlic cloves, peeled and thinly sliced

1 square inch root ginger, peeled and finely
   chopped

250 ml (8 fl oz) chicken stock

1 glass red wine

Light soy sauce

4 star anise

Preheat the oven to 180°C/350°F/gas mark 4. Brown the duck legs in a hot dry pan. You won't need any oil as they will produce sufficient fat of their own. Transfer these to a baking tray and drizzle over the honey and sprinkle on the Five-Spice powder. Tip most of the fat from the first pan and then add the garlic and ginger and sauté gently for a few minutes until just beginning to soften. Add the liquids and the star anise and bring to the boil, then simmer for 5 minutes before pouring round the duck legs and sealing with a double layer of foil. Roast in the oven for an hour then remove the foil and increase the heat for 15 minutes or so just to crisp the skin if wished.

Serve with a salad of chicory, watercress, red onion and pear, dressed with some lemon juice and olive oil.

Duck with Hedgerow Sauce

Should you happen to have wild mallard to hand, then try them with this sauce which is a perfect foil to the dark, rich meat. One bird is sufficient for two people. If not, then use magret du canard (breasts of duck).

3 magret du canard	1 glass red wine
150 ml (¼ pint) chicken stock	100 g (4 oz) ripe blackberries
1 tablespoon red or blackcurrant jelly	Seasoning

Score the fat on the duck breasts in a lattice pattern. Cook these by placing them on a rack set over a tin either under a hot grill or in the oven at 200°C/400°F/gas mark 6 for approximately 12–14 minutes then leave to rest in a warm place.

For the sauce, reduce the stock by half, then add the jelly and dissolve over the heat. Pour in the red wine and reduce again before tipping in the blackberries and, if too sweet, add a spritz of lemon juice. Additonally, a splash of Ribena or even cassis can taste very good in this if there is some to hand.

To serve, carve the duck breasts diagonally and pour on the sauce. A purée of potatoes and celeriac is good with this.

Tip from the Sink ∼

Try also substituting half the quantity of blackberries for elderberries. The easiest way of removing the elderberries from their stalks is by holding them in one hand and running the prongs of a fork downwards to strip them off. This method also works brilliantly for red and white currants as well as for detaching thyme leaves from their rather brittle stems.

Duck with Glazed Turnips and Honey

The humble turnip, like so many of its other root counterparts, is often overlooked when it comes to choice of vegetables. It makes a natural ally to rich casseroles and game dishes as well as to this duck.

3 large duck breasts, fat scored
450 g (1 lb) small turnips
300 ml (½ pint) chicken stock
Olive oil

2 tablespoons honey
50 g (2 oz) butter
Splash of Madeira

Preheat the oven to 180°C/350°F/gas mark 4. Begin by peeling and quartering the turnips then blanche them in boiling water. Place the peelings in a saucepan together with the chicken stock and reduce the liquid by half then remove the peelings. Whisk in the butter, season to taste then add the Madeira and a squeeze of lemon juice. If it needs to be a little sweeter, add a little honey. This can be prepared ahead and left to sit.

Heat a slick of olive oil in a baking tray and when sizzling, add the turnips and roast in the oven. After approximately 15 minutes, turn them and add the honey, returning them to the heat to glaze and go brown.

Meanwhile, heat the grill and cook the duck breasts on a rack for approximately 12–14 minutes or roast in the oven for a similar period of time. Remove, cover and rest in a warm place.

To serve, carve the duck meat into diagonal slices and surround with the turnips then pour over some of the sauce.

Meat

Whether it is lamb, beef, veal or pork, the rules remain the same when buying meat. Provenance is vital so always source the finest produce from a reliable supplier. There can be no substitute when it comes to flavour and tenderness for carefully reared and, wherever and whenever possible, local animals which have enjoyed a stress free life and are then hung for a proper period of time, i.e. a minimum of twenty-one days. As far as red meat is concerned, what you want is deep, dark coloured meat with a marbling of fat and, the blacker it is, then the longer it has been hanging. As all astute cooks know, forking out huge sums of money for the most expensive cut of meat alone does not guarantee you the most superb results. Remember, also, to make use of the less expensive and fashionable parts of a beast including offal and even its blood which is a star ingredient in delicacies such as black pudding.

The true art of cooking meat is to remember always to bring it to room temperature before putting it into the oven, to baste it frequently whilst it is cooking and then to rest it really well afterwards. Because I only have a very ancient two-oven Aga (the bottom part of which is scarcely warmer than 100°C/220°F/gas mark ¼) I often cook a large joint, e.g. a leg of lamb before even starting on the other ingredients and leave it to stand, well wrapped in foil and a blanket or towel for up to two hours. Decent insulation will ensure it remains perfectly hot for an amazingly long period of time. The longer the meat is rested for, the braver you dare to be about 'undercooking' it – safe in the knowledge that the heat within it during the time it was in the oven will continue to 'cook' it on. As the meat relaxes and tenderises, then so the carving of it becomes easier. The only other issue, of course, is for how long to cook meat. If, like me, you enjoy steak tartare and carpaccio then you will err towards less cooking time. Trying to please everyone can be difficult so follow my rule which is, when at home, I cook my meat how I like to eat it and, when dining at someone else's table, then I happily eat whatever they produce – even if it is nearing the cremation stage!

Roast Belly of Pork with Raisin and Cider Sauce

This cheap cut of meat is enjoying cult status on the list of 'in-vogue' foods. It makes the perfect Sunday lunch and a whole belly will feed twelve people comfortably and economically, though it will shrink considerably during cooking time. A large oven is the main requirement which makes an Aga ideal. The trick is to make sure the skin is well scored and to roast it slowly either on either a rack or a bed of halved but not skinned onions which will be deliciously sweet.

SERVES 10–12
One whole belly of pork
Cooking apples, cored

For the Sauce
4 tablespoons brown sugar
1½ tablespoon cornflour
½ teaspoon salt

Small bottle dry cider (I use Katy!)
2 tablespoons chicken stock
Sticks of cinnamon
3 tablespoons raisins
1 small onion, peeled and studded
   with whole cloves

Preheat the oven to 160°C/325°F/gas mark 3. Place the pork on a large rack over a roasting tin and cook for a minimum of 3½–4 hours until the crackling is wonderfully crisp and crunchy.

Using a sharp knife, score the apples around their circumference and stand in a tray containing some water. Bake for approximately 50 minutes until soft to the touch.

For the sauce, combine the sugar, cornflour and salt in a bowl and mix to a smooth paste with a little of the cider. Transfer to a saucepan and add the stock, raisins, onion and cinnamon and cook for 10 minutes. Remove the cinammon and serve hot with the pork.

Tip from the Sink ~

This sauce can also be served with baked ham.

Pork Tenderloin with Flageolet Beans and a Tarragon Cream Sauce

An easy dish for entertaining purposes.

2 tenderloin fillets of pork
Prunes, pitted and ready soaked
Sage leaves
Olive oil
Butter

For the Sauce
300 ml (½ pint) chicken stock
1 glass Noilly Prat or white wine
3 tablespoons crème fraîche
Seasoning
Handful tarragon leaves, finely chopped

Preheat the oven to 190°C/375°F/gas mark 5. Run the blade of a sharp knife down the centre of each pork fillet (or ask your butcher to do this for you) and lay them open. Stuff the centre with the prunes and sage leaves then season, roll up and secure with string. Heat some olive oil and butter in a pan and, when sizzling, seal the fillets until the entire surface is nicely browned. (This will only take a couple of minutes.) Cook in the oven for approximately 15 minutes then remove, cover and keep warm.

For the sauce: put the stock in a saucepan and reduce down by half. Add the alcohol and reduce again so it just thickens slightly. Add the crème fraîche and whisk in. Season. Leave to one side and, just before serving, stir in the tarragon.

Slice the pork fillets and arrange on a bed of flageolet beans which have been tipped into a sieve and rinsed through with boiling water. For extra colour, add some oven roasted cherry tomatoes, cooked peas or beans. Spoon over a little of the sauce and hand round the rest separately.

Herb Crusted Rack of Lamb

2 racks of lamb, trimmed and French
    chined (6–7 cutlets on each)
English mustard

Herb crust
4–5 slices slightly stale white bread, crusts
    removed

Large handful each parsley, marjoram,
    thyme and tarragon leaves
50 g (2 oz) butter
Seasoning

Preheat the oven to 200°C/400°F/gas mark 6. Process the bread until crumbed then add the herbs and seasoning and whiz again. Melt the butter and pour this in to bind the mixture.

Score the lamb fat and smear with a little mustard then press on the herbs and bread-crumbs.

Place in a baking tray and cook for approximately 20 minutes then rest before serving with something simple such as melted redcurrant jelly. Carve each rack into individual cutlets – no one wants a great dollop of meat landing on their plate!

Loin of Lamb with Sauce Provençale

1 best-end loin of lamb, boned then
    trimmed and secured with string
Sprigs rosemary
Olive oil
Butter
Seasoning

For the Sauce
250 g (8 oz) vine cherry tomatoes
1 teaspoon sherry vinegar
1 teaspoon caster sugar
1 tablespoon basil leaves, chopped
2–3 tablespoons chicken stock
50 g (2 oz) butter, cold cubes
Handful stoned olives, thinly sliced
    crossways

Preheat the oven to 190°C/375°F/gas mark 5. Season the lamb and heat the oil and butter in a roasting pan and sear the meat briefly on all sides to brown, tuck the rosemary around it then transfer to the oven and cook for 15 minutes. Remove from the heat, cover and keep warm.

To make the sauce, halve the tomatoes and whiz with the vinegar, sugar and basil in a processor, then sieve. Cook for approximately 10 minutes until reduced by half and quite pulpy. Add the stock, heat through then whisk in the cubes of butter thoroughly to give it a glossy sheen. Check seasoning and toss in the olives.

Carve the lamb into noisettes or thin slices (whichever you prefer) and serve with roasted new potatoes and chunks of aubergine griddled in olive oil until nicely crisped.

Jonathan's Lamb

This came about by a quirky fate. I had cooked two legs of finest spring lamb for dinner following a Domestic God's Demo and ended up, as inevitably happens, with some meat on both joints. It seemed a shame to turn it into the standard shepherd's pie and it was Jonathan who suggested making it into a very mild sort of curry but, when I questioned him as to what might go into it, he was suitably vague. Determined, nevertheless, to give it a go, the end result seemed to get the green light. It's a great way of turning leftovers into something less routine than the usual hash-up.

1 kg (2¼ lbs) cooked lamb, cubed
500 ml (16 oz) pot of Greek yoghurt
1 bunch spring onions, white part only,
    finely chopped crossways
Clove of garlic, crushed
1 square inch root ginger, peeled and
    grated
Small red chilli, seeded and minutely diced
400 ml (14 oz) tin coconut milk

1 tablespoon soft brown sugar
1 tablespoon cardamon powder
Juice of a lime
100 g (4 oz) ready-to-eat apricots
Handful mint leaves, roughly chopped
Handful coriander leaves, roughly chopped
2 tablespoons flaked almonds, lightly
    toasted

Begin by lining a sieve with a J-cloth, balance this over a bowl then decant the yoghurt into this and leave in the fridge overnight so that all the liquid drains off into the bowl beneath. This is then discarded

Put the spring onions, garlic, ginger and chilli into a large frying pan and add a little of the coconut milk then simmer until everything is soft. Add the rest of the tin of milk plus the yoghurt and bring to the boil. Stir in the sugar, cardamon and the lime juice then toss in the meat and heat through together with the apricots and half the quantity of both the mint and coriander leaves.

Arrange cooked Pink Fir Apple potatoes on a large warmed plate, pile on the lamb and finish by scattering over the remaining herbs and the toasted almonds.

Casteroled Lamb with Tomato and Pesto

This recipe belongs to Claire MacDonald of MacDonald, distinguished cookery writer, and it's a King amongst Casseroles. Rich without being too heavy, it reaches the higher echelons of wholesome cooking making it good enough to serve not just for hearty lunches but worthy also of elegant dinners. Make it, cook it and then reheat so the flavours can really develop.

1.3 kg (3 lb) lamb, cut into 1 inch chunks and trimmed of excessive fat

2 tablespoons plain flour

3 tablespoons olive oil

2 medium onions, skinned and finely sliced

2 garlic cloves, finely chopped

2 x 400 g (15 oz) tins tomatoes

285 ml (½ pint) white wine

Pinch sugar, salt and freshly ground pepper

2–3 large tablespoons pesto sauce

Season the flour with salt and pepper and toss the lamb pieces in it. Heat the olive oil in a heavy casserole and brown the lamb all over, a few pieces at a time. Set aside. Add the onions and garlic to the oil (you may need a tad more) and meat juices and sauté for approximately 5 minutes until soft and translucent. Next, add the tomatoes; breaking them up with a wooden spoon against the side of the pan. Stir in the white wine, sugar and pesto, season and bring *gently* to the boil, just! Return the meat to the casserole, cover with a lid and put in the oven at 190°C/375°F/gas mark 5 for at least 1½ hours.

Like all casseroles, this one tastes best if reheated the following day before serving. Eat with tagliatelle, which has been tossed in olive oil, and some freshly grated Parmesan cheese, and a green salad.

Fillet of Beef with Béarnaise Sauce

This most poetic of foods unfailingly satisfies the cravings of the most devoted carnivores. The sauce is a speciality of Béarn, a region where the cuisine is rich and luxurious. A fast, failsafe method, Béarnaise should never be served hot, only tepid, hence it can be made in advance.

1 fillet of beef, trimmed and tied up
Olive oil
Butter
Few sprigs thyme
Seasoning

For the Sauce
3 egg yolks
2 teaspoons dried tarragon

Splash tarragon vinegar
175 g (6 oz) butter, cubed
Squeeze lemon juice
1 tablespoon fresh tarragon leaves,
   chopped
Seasoning

Place the egg yolks in a bowl and sit it over a pan of boiling water, making sure the base of the bowl does not touch the water. Add the dried herbs and vinegar and combine. Whisk in the butter, one cube at a time, making sure each piece has been absorbed into the sauce before continuing. Season, add lemon juice and to finish, stir in the fresh tarragon leaves.

Preheat the oven to 190°C/375°F/gas mark 5. Season the fillet, heat the oil and butter in a roasting tin and when sizzling, swiftly sear the meat on all sides until nicely browned. This gives it a good sharp injection of heat which helps with the cooking. Transfer to the oven and cook for approximately 15–20 minutes depending on how rare you like your fillet to be. Remove from the heat, cover and rest for at least another 20 minutes before carving.

Cauliflower Cheese Cottage Pie

As a child I loathed mince. My first school, run by the redoubtable Miss Booth, had no kitchen so we all took our own packed lunches. As at picnics when everyone else's spread always looks so much more enticing than one's own, so the containers belonging to others appeared vastly more tempting than mine. My mother took a dim view of cold foods during the winter months and I was sent off with a red, wide-necked thermos full of steaming mince. Somehow the resultant smell and taste were so incredibly nasty I always tipped it down the loo. Thereafter, it took many years of non-thermos mince to make me realise what I had been missing.

This falls into what my son Fred and I call our 'Slump/Slop Suppers' category. In other words, it is perfect food at the end of a long day when what you really crave is something deliciously old-fashioned and comforting which can be forked effortlessly into the mouth. That said, however, it's great also for winter parties such as Bonfire Night, with steaming, baked potatoes.

675 g (1½ lbs) beef mince – either fresh or
    leftovers from a joint
2 medium onions, peeled and finely
    chopped
Olive oil
300 ml (½ pint) liquid, i.e. red wine, stock
    or gravy
1 x 400 g (14 oz) tin plum tomatoes
1 teaspoon Bovril
Few shakes Worcester sauce
Gloop tomato ketchup
1 tablespoon thyme leaves
Bay leaf

Seasoning
1 medium cauliflower
Bay leaf

For the Sauce
300 ml (½ pint) milk
25 g (1 oz) plain flour
40 g (1½ oz) butter
1 teaspoon English mustard
Rasping grated nutmeg
Seasoning
75 g (3 oz) mature cheddar cheese, grated

Break the cauliflower into florets and cook in a pan of salted boiling water along with the bay leaf which helps allay the cabbage-like aroma! When just tender (no more) drain quickly.

For the sauce, put everything bar the cheese into a saucepan and whisk over the heat until smooth and thickened then stir in the cheese to melt before seasoning.

For the mince, preheat the oven to 180°C/350°F/gas mark 4. In a large pan cook the onions in the oil until soft and translucent then add the mince. Stir well and pour on a little of the liquid and leave to simmer for 5 minutes before adding the remaining ingredients. Cover with a lid and cook in the oven for at least 1½ hours in the usual way, then transfer to a large ovenproof dish.

To finish off, place the cauliflower on top of the minced beef then coat with the sauce. Top with a sprinkling of breadcrumbs or a little more cheese and cook in the oven for around 15 minutes until just browned and bubbling.

Tip from the Sink ⁓

Replace the cauliflower and beef mince with leeks and lamb.

Roast Loin of Veal

Many meat-eaters I know claim not to approve of veal. If they will forgive me for saying so this is mostly due to ignorance. Taking the moral high ground is fine providing the dissentient has done their homework and can supply the evidence. So, I beg to differ and ask: what can possibly be perceived as cruel about veal calves that are reared with their mothers in their natural surroundings, i.e. fields, fed on milk and hay and kept until they are at least five months old? Once again, it's all about good husbandry and a proper butcher!

SERVES 8

1.2 kg (2½ lbs) boned and rolled loin of veal

Olive oil

2 tins anchovies, drained

2–3 shallots, peeled

4 garlic cloves, split in half

Few sprigs rosemary

350 ml (12 fl oz) Vermouth/Noilly Prat

350 ml (12 fl oz) chicken stock

Seasoning

Preheat the oven to 150°C/300°F/gas mark 2. Dry heat a large pan or roasting tin. Rub the joint with the olive oil and brown all over, turning several times so that it cooks evenly. Make slits in the meat and push in the anchovies then add the remaining ingredients and season the meat but use very little salt. Cover with foil and roast in the oven for 2½ hours until done, then remove, cover and leave to rest in a warm place. Carve and serve, very simply, with the juices in the pan.

Puddings

$\mathcal{F}$OND AS I AM OF PUDDINGS, I seldom eat them during the week since I invariably seem to have run out of time, stamina or space (or all three). And that is their one drawback coming, as they do, after everything else. They remain, therefore, something
of an indulgence and are reserved either for Sunday lunch, a special celebration or simply for those occasions when I am feeling exceptionally hungry (or greedy!).

The point about producing puddings is to remain unpressurised. There is nothing worse than the host who inflicts 'trolley torture' upon guests by trotting out an unending selection of puddings and takes it as a personal insult when all are politely declined. A laid-back approach is far better; after all, if the French, with all their savoir faire, are happy to buy a tarte from their local patisserie, then why shouldn't we adopt the same practice? Alternatively two, or at most three, carefully selected cheeses, each one presented in perfect condition, along with a jug of celery or a plateful of fresh and dried organic fruits will not incur any complaints.

Hours spent worrying over baskets of spun sugar so delicate they break if one breathes on them or assembling intricately layered creations of architectural dimensions are just not my style. Hence this chapter reflects my love of simpler puddings often jazzed up with a modest twist. Ice creams, crumbles, quivering jellies plus a few wickedly rich chocolate splurges are all firm favourites but supreme amongst them all are those fruit-orientated treats: whether its strawberries in lime syrup for a refreshing summer finale or a baked Seville sponge with thick cream to counter the cold on a winter's day. One point I should emphasise when making puddings is that, rather like baking cakes and biscuits, they do call for a degree of accuracy when weighing out quantities.

Rhubarb, Ginger and Orange Crumble

Look out for the early forced jewel-pink stems of rhubarb which appear in January (so much better than those chunky and unfailingly stringy later-season stalks). They can be transformed into wonderful fools, tarts, syllabubs, jams, ice creams or meringue topped pies as well as into this rich crumble. Rhubarb shares a natural affinity with ginger and orange.

750 g (1¾ lbs) trimmed rhubarb	*For the Crumble*
2 lumps stem ginger, sliced into thin julienne, and a little syrup	175 g (6 oz) digestive, ginger nut or Hobnob biscuits
Grated zest of an orange	100 g (4 oz) butter
75 g (3 oz) soft brown sugar	100 g (4 oz) demerara sugar

Preheat the oven to 180°C/350°F/gas mark 4. Cut the rhubarb into 3 cm/1 inch lengths and combine in a bowl together with the sugar, ginger plus syrup and orange zest. Transfer the ingredients to a suitable ovenproof dish.

For the crumble, put the biscuits into a strong polythene bag, beat with a rolling pin to crush into crumbs, though make sure they retain some texture and are not reduced to sand. Melt the butter in a pan, add the sugar and biscuit crumbs and stir well to combine, adding a pinch of powdered ginger if you wish. Pile on top of the fruit and spread out evenly then bake in the oven for 35–40 minutes until the top is golden brown and the juices have just begun to bubble through the surface. Serve, in time-honoured fashion, with home-made custard.

Sticky Toffee Pudding

An indisputable winter winner.

175 g (6 oz) stoneless dates
300 ml (½ pint) boiling water
1 teaspoon bicarbonate of soda
50 g (2 oz) butter
175 g (6 oz) golden caster or soft brown
    sugar
175 g (6 oz) self-raising flour

2 eggs
½ teaspoon vanilla essence

For the Sauce
200 g (7 oz) dark brown Muscovado sugar
100 g (4 oz) butter
½ teaspoon vanilla essence
6 tablespoons double cream

Preheat the oven to 180°C/350°F/gas mark 4. For the pudding, put the dates into a saucepan with the water and bring to the boil. Remove from the heat and stir in the bicarbonate of soda then leave to stand for 10 minutes. Cream together the butter, caster sugar, eggs, flour and vanilla essence and add this to the dates. Spoon into a lightly buttered shallow baking dish and bake for approximately 50 minutes.

To make the sauce, put all the ingredients in a saucepan, stir and bring to the boil. Serve with thick cream.

Tip from the Sink ～

I always make this beforehand, pierce the top of the sponge with a skewer and pour over some sauce then return to the oven for 10 minutes or so when ready to serve.

Seville Orange Sponge

A zesty first cousin to Lemon Surprise Pudding, and far less of a sweat to cook than a steamed sponge. In the unlikely event of there being any leftovers, they taste just as good when eaten cold.

4 large eggs, separated	175 g (6 oz) caster sugar
2 Seville oranges, grated zest and juice	475 ml (16 fl oz) milk
25 g (1 oz) butter	2–3 tablespoons marmalade, optional
50 g (2 oz) plain flour	

Preheat the oven to 180°C/350°F/gas mark 4. Butter a 1.5 litre (2½ pint) ovenproof dish. Put the egg yolks, sugar, butter, flour, orange zest and juice into a processor and blend. Add the milk through the funnel and mix until smooth. Beat the egg whites until stiff in a large clean bowl and fold the liquid into these. It will seem unbelievably sloppy but don't be alarmed!

Spread the marmalade, if using, over the base of the dish and pour the mixture over. Stand in a roasting tin and half fill with boiling water. Place in the centre of the oven for approximately 30–35 minutes until the sponge is just firm to the touch and a skewer, when inserted, comes out clean. Remove from the oven and the bain-marie and serve either hot or cold.

Tip from the Sink ~

This pudding may also be made with ordinary oranges, lemons or limes or even a combination.

Fudgey Fruit

There is nothing more compelling than a delicious butterscotch-style sauce – and never mind the calories. It is excellent with bullet-like fruit which refuses to ripen such as nectarines or pears – simply skin, or peel then stone or core as appropriate and slice up. It's also good with bananas and ice cream.

175 g (6 oz) soft brown sugar
100 g (4 oz) butter
Few drops vanilla essence
225 ml (7 fl oz) double cream

Put everything into a saucepan, heat through gently until the butter and sugar are melted and dissolved then bring to the boil, stirring well. Leave to cool a little before pouring over the fruit. This sauce can also be stored in the fridge for up to five days but it will solidify so either reheat or bring back to room temperature (stand near the Aga) to serve.

Hot Chocolate Fondant Puddings

100 g (4 oz) butter	2 whole eggs + 2 yolks
Extra butter and cocoa powder to grease ramekins	125 g (5 oz) caster sugar
	100 g (4 oz) plain flour
100 g (4 oz) dark chocolate, over 70% cocoa content	4 dessertspoons marmalade or stem ginger to taste, cut into fine julienne

Heat the oven to 160°C/325°F/gas mark 3. Butter four large ramekin dishes then dust with cocoa powder. Melt the chocolate and butter together in a saucepan (or in a bowl placed on the Aga) then leave to cool for 10 minutes.

Whisk up the eggs and yolks with the sugar until pale and creamy then add the liquid chocolate and butter. Sift the flour over the mixture and gently fold in with a metal spoon. Put a dollop into each ramekin, then the marmalade and/or ginger followed by the rest of the chocolate mixture.

Cook for approximately 12 minutes or so, then turn out onto plates, dust with icing sugar and serve at once.

Tip from the Sink ∼

The inclusion of some marmalade and/or stem ginger is very good with the chocolate.

Roasted Pineapple, Pain Perdu with Mascarpone and Kirsch

Obviously you can simplify this by just slicing your pineapple – which must be ripe – dusting it with sieved icing sugar and pouring over some kirsch. Should you feel so inclined, however, then this pudding is well worth the extra effort.

1 large ripe pineapple, skin removed, cut into slices and each one quartered
100 g (4 oz) butter
3–4 tablespoons icing sugar, plus extra to dust
2 eggs, beaten

4 slices brioche bread
1–2 tablespoons sunflower or groundnut oil
Mascarpone cheese
Kirsch

Heat half the butter in a griddle pan and toss in the pineapple. Sprinkle with icing sugar and continue to cook over a high heat until nicely caramelised – approximately 4–5 minutes. Remove the fruit, keep it warm and wipe out the pan.

Pour the beaten eggs into a shallow dish and dip a slice of brioche into it, turn and coat the other side then heat the rest of the butter and the oil in the pan and, when hot, fry the bread briefly on both sides until golden brown. Remove and keep warm, repeating the process with the rest of the bread. As soon as they are all done, place each slice on a plate and spoon the fruit on top. Add a scoop of mascarpone cheese mix with a little kirsch to each one. To gild the lily, decorate with a vanilla pod, dusted with icing sugar.

Tip from the Sink ～

This works just as well with apples, pears and plums.
Try, also, a trickle of maple syrup over the fruit.

Cheat's Crêpes Suzette

Nothing beats the theatre of these flambéed in front of the restaurant diner and, when at home, there's something very therapeutic about making one's own crêpes or pancakes, once the first one (always a disaster in my experience) has been successfully dispensed with. Thereafter, the pan seems to have heated up, is coated with just enough fat and is ready for action. When time is short, however, have a supermarket brand of ready-mades, usually eight to a pack, to hand!

For the Filling	Grated zest of an orange
100 g (4 oz) butter	1 glass Grand Marnier or
100 g (4 oz) icing sugar	Cointreau

Preheat the oven to 180°C/350°F/gas mark 4. Whizz the butter and icing sugar together with the orange zest and half the orange liqueur. Divide the mixture between the pancakes, fold each one in half then in half again, to form triangles. Butter a shallow ovenproof dish and lay the crêpes, slightly overlapping, within.

Bake in the oven for 15–20 minutes until the buttery filling has melted and the pancakes are hot. Warm the rest of the alcohol in a small pan, ignite, then pour over the dish. Serve with pouring cream.

Fig and Walnut Tart

Of course you can make your own pastry if you wish, but I am a big fan of ready-made dessert pastry which, when rolled out in icing sugar rather than ordinary flour, is deliciously sweet.

375 g (12 oz) packet Saxby's dessert pastry	2250 g (8 oz) butter
3 tablespoons raspberry jam, warmed	75 g (3 oz) granulated sugar
250 g (8 oz) walnuts	3 eggs, beaten
4–6 ripe, fresh figs	1 teaspoon vanilla essence
50 g (2 oz) plain flour	Icing sugar, for dusting

Preheat the oven to 180°C/350°F/gas mark 4. Roll out the pasty on a lightly icing sugared surface and line a 25 cm (10 inch) tin with a removeable base. Prick the dough with a fork and refrigerate for 30 minutes (or put in the deep-freeze for 10–15 minutes) then bake blind for approximately 15 minutes. Just before it is done, remove the paper and beans and return to the oven to let the base crisp up. Leave to cool then spread the bottom with the raspberry jam.

Meanwhile, whizz the nuts briefly until roughly chopped then add the flour and grind quickly to a fine mixture but don't overdo as the nuts become oily and the flavour is tainted. Quarter the figs.

Cream the butter and sugar together until pale and fluffy. Beat in the eggs and vanilla essence and then fold in the nut mixture. Spoon into the pastry case and arrange the figs in a flower pattern on top. Bake in the oven for approximately 50 minutes until the sponge is just springy to the touch. If it begins to take on too much colour, cover with a double layer of greaseproof paper. The juice from the figs may have started to seep out slightly but don't be alarmed. Leave to cool then dust with sieved icing sugar.

Tip from the Sink ∼

Omit the figs if not available.

Tarte Tatin

This was the first 'proper' pudding I ever attempted and it has remained a firm favourite ever since. It's an upside-down apple pie and the French call it tarte des demoiselles Tatin – *the tart of two spinster sisters. It is traditionally made in a copper pan but I use a very old, cast iron frying pan which works perfectly well. You just need something which conducts the heat adequately so avoid tinny or wobbly tins! Pears are good in this too.*

450 g (1 lb) puff pastry (I always use readymade)

10–12 firm eating apples, e.g. Granny Smiths, large Cox's, Royal Worcester

100–150 g (4–6 oz) butter

75–100 g (3–4 oz) caster sugar

1 teaspoon cinnamon powder

Start by slicing the butter into thin slivers and cover the base of the pan with these, then hide them under a blanket of sugar! Peel, core and quarter the apples and arrange these (upright) in concentric circles inside the pan, making sure they are as tightly packed as possible. Put on the top of the stove and cook slowly for at least 40 minutes or until the butter and sugar have turned a dark caramel colour and look like toffee – but you must not let it burn. This is quite a slow process and you need to exercise patience! Sprinkle over the cinnamon powder.

Roll out the puff pastry to a thickness of around a £1 coin. Lay over the fruit covering the apples comfortably with a generous overhang. (Reserve the leftovers for use another time – it freezes well.) Stand the pan on a baking sheet and put in the oven for approximately 15–20 minutes until the pastry is nicely puffed up and golden. Remove and leave to stand for at least 15 minutes to allow the caramel on the base to set.

When ready to serve, run a palette knife around the edge of the tin and invert onto a large round plate, giving it a good shake. Pray for a perfect turnout but don't panic if one or two pieces of fruit refuse to budge. Simply piece them together with the rest and no one will be any the wiser!

Meringues Mont Blanc

As a small child the sheer drag of going to London was instantly ameliorated by a visit to the Soda Fountain in Fortnum & Mason. My order never changed – Welsh 'rabbit' with apples followed by their house speciality Mont Blanc meringues. A life-saver for the starved schoolchild!

Meringues satisfy the cravings of even the most sweet-toothed person. I always think that the more home-made these chalky confections look the better they are so, for that reason, I never use a piping bag when making them but just spoon blobs out onto the baking sheet. Sometimes, for extra marsh-mallowy gooeyness and a bit of colour, I make them using brown sugar, or even half and half.

4 egg whites	400 g (14 oz) tin unsweetened
225 g (8 oz) caster sugar	chestnut purée
1 teaspoon cornflour	300 ml (½ pint) double cream,
1 teaspoon white wine vinegar	whipped and sweetened

Preheat the oven to 110°C/225°F/gas mark ¼. Whisk the whites stiffly and gradually fold in the sugar, a spoonful at a time, until perfectly glossy. Using a large metal spoon, mix in the cornflour and white wine vinegar. Line a baking sheet with either a sheet of oiled greaseproof paper or a sheet of Bake-o-Glide and drop spoonfuls on it. Bake for approximately 3–4 hours until very lightly coloured or lower the temperature after the first hour to 75°C/160°F and leave overnight.

Push the chestnut purée through the holes of a colander, or potato ricer if you happen to have one, straight on to the flat side of the meringues so that it falls in little worms. Top with a cap of the cream and sandwich together with another meringue.

Soft Chocolate Cake

*My son Fred is something of an aficionado when it comes to chocolate, and that's official.
Over the years, we've scrutinised countless recipes and eaten our way through every sort
of cake. This one, though, ticks all the boxes, being Rich, Dark and Handsome, and it
also makes a wonderful pudding. During the winter, I serve it with poached kumquats
and in the summer it goes especially well with raspberries or a compôte of stoned cherries.*

225 g (8 oz) good quality plain chocolate,
minimum 70% cocoa solids

225 g (8 oz) butter

150g (5 oz) caster sugar

6 whole eggs

2 egg whites

Preheat the oven to 160°C/325°F/gas mark 3. Melt the chocolate and butter together –
either in a bowl over a pan of simmering water or by leaving to stand on the side of
the Aga. Process the sugar and egg yolks until pale and thick, then fold into the melted
chocolate.

Whisk the egg whites until just stiff then fold in the chocolate mixture. Turn into a
well-buttered loose-based cake tin and bake in the oven for approximately 45 minutes then
remove and leave to cool. When completely cold, turn out onto a plate, dust with sieved
icing sugar and/or cocoa powder.

Eton Mess

New tyres on old wheels – here are two different ways of presenting this versatile pudding.

SERVES 6

350 g (12 oz) ripe strawberries

2 tablespoons caster sugar

Squeeze lemon juice

300 ml (½ pint) double cream

75 g (3 oz) icing sugar

3–4 crushed meringues

250–275 g (8–10 oz) mixed summer berries

Blend the strawberries together with the sugar and lemon juice then pass through a sieve. Beat the cream with the icing sugar just until it thickens (you do not want to it to become too solid) then fold in the meringues and divide the mixture equally between four suitable glasses. Mix the berries into the strawberry purée and spoon on top of the cream mixture.

This alternative method comes from Catherine Chichester and is a great standby to have in the deep-freeze when ice cream is called for! Make a raspberry coulis by heating the berries in a pan together with soft brown sugar (just enough to sweeten). Pass through a sieve. Whisk double cream until stiff, fold in some strawberries which have been mashed with a fork and some crushed meringues then add half the raspberry coulis. Stir only briefly otherwise you will destroy that marbled effect. Freeze in a bowl and remove at least 25 minutes before you wish to serve it. Unmould and pour the remaining sauce over the top.

Tip from the Sink ～

Make use of other fruits, such as blackberries or poached rhubarb – according to what is in season.

Strawberries in Lime Syrup

Limes are wonderfully refreshing and this combo eclipses strawberries and cream every time.

300 ml (½ pint) water	Juice of 3 limes
200 g (7 oz) caster sugar	2 large punnets ripe
Zest of 7 limes	strawberries, hulled

Put the first three ingredients into a pan and bring to the boil. Remove from the heat and add the lime juice. Cover and leave to infuse overnight then strain and pour over sliced strawberries.

Cherries with White Chocolate Dipping Sauce

225 g (8 oz) good quality white chocolate

200 g (7 oz) tub mascarpone cheese

2 tablespoons crème fraîche

Single cream

Melt the chocolate then mix in the cheese and crème fraîche. Be careful not to overbeat or it can 'split'. Add single cream until the desired consistency is reached. Spoon over the fruit or serve in a ramekin and just plunge the berries into this.

Tip from the Sink ∼

Dried lavender stalks may be used as kebabs upon which to thread a selection of summer fruits and berries. Fan out on a large platter around a bowl of the chocolate dip.

Elderflower Jelly with Summer Fruits

I make this in an old-fashioned jelly mould then turn it out and fill the centre with scoops of ice cream or yet more soft summer fruits.

1 litre (1¾ pints) elderflower cordial –
diluted with water to appropriate
strength

8½ leaves gelatine (or 4 whole sheets)

350 g (12 oz) mixed summer berries –
I use blueberries, strawberries and
raspberries

Begin by soaking the gelatine leaves in a bowl of cold water and leave them to stand for at least 10 minutes until totally soft and spongy. Make up the elderflower liquid. Squeeze out the water from the gelatine and either melt in a small saucepan over a gentle heat or leave to stand in a bowl on the side of the Aga until clear and liquid. Stir into the elderflower. Fill a jelly mould (or suitable bowl) with cold water then tip out and immediately pour in a quarter of the elderflower liquid. Dot around a quarter of the fruit and put into the fridge until just set. Repeat the process and allow the next layer to set before continuing until all the liquid and fruits have been used up.

To serve, remove the jelly from the fridge and leave to stand at room temperature for approximately 5 minutes then run a palette knife around the mould and invert on to a plate.

Tip from the Sink ～

Leaf gelatine is far superior to powder sachets which lack the clarity and tend to possess a rather nasty glue-like taste.

Ice Bowl

This is well worth the effort, guarantees the 'wow' factor and, when rinsed out and returned immediately after use to the deep-freeze, can be recycled at least five or six times! Make use of whatever is growing in the hedgerows (according to the time of year), as well as the garden, to decorate.

Two china or glass bowls – one approximately 2½ cm (1 inch) larger all round than the other	Ice cubes
	Cold water
	Flowers and foliage as filling

The only tricky part is the first bit – balancing the smaller bowl inside the larger one on a bed of ice so that it is sitting reasonably centrally. Fill the base of the larger bowl with ice cubes and sit the smaller one on top then pour in a little water (I find a small watering can with a long spout especially useful for this) then transfer swiftly to the deep-freeze making sure you place it on a level surface so the whole thing doesn't topple sideways. Leave for 10–15 minutes to start to freeze. Once iced, push some flowers and/or leaves into the gap all the way round them and cover with water. Freeze once again and repeat the exercise. The object is to pack the space between the two bowls with suitable blooms and greenery. When completed, leave to set for at least 6 hours – or preferably overnight – then unmould. Fill the centre of the inner bowl with hand hot water (boiling hot will crack the ice). Leave for a few minutes and wiggle a bit to loosen. A palette knife can be quite handy here. Lift out the inner bowl then stand the main bowl in a basin of hand-hot water. After a couple of minutes it is possible to slip away the main bowl. Stand the ice bowl immediately on a linen napkin and place on a plate then return to the freezer until ready to use.

Tip from the sink ∿

Autumn and winter berries – e.g. hips and holly – look spectacular when used in ice bowls.

Instant Iced Delights

Wild and wacky; fun 'n' funky. Here's an 'assembly job' suggestion – great for a party, especially when you want to save on the washing up.

> 1 kg (2¼ lb) bag unrefined caster/granulated sugar
> Shop-bought ice cream cones
> Selection of ice creams or sorbets in contrasting colours

Fill a deep-sided bowl, preferably glass, with the sugar then wedge the cones, filled with either ice creams or sorbets, upright in it – as if putting a spade into the sand. That's it! Hand round and let everyone help themselves.

Tip from the Sink ∿

Soften some ordinary vanilla ice cream and then add pieces of chopped chocolate bars – such as KitKats, Maltesers, Crunchies or Dime bars – then return to the freezer until required.

Strawberry Tart

Not only does this look pretty as a picture, but it also tastes marvellous.

SERVES 8

350 g (12 oz) packet dessert pastry

1 egg white

150 g (5 oz) quality white chocolate

200 g (7 oz) mascarpone cheese

Small tub crème fraîche

Grated zest ½ lemon or ½ orange

450 g (1 lb) hulled strawberries, halved

Icing sugar

Preheat the oven to 180°C/350°F/gas mark 4. Roll out the pastry on a flat surface dusted with icing sugar and line a 25 cm (10 inch) tart tin with a removeable base. Prick all over and refrigerate for 30 minutes. Bake blind for 15 minutes then remove the beans and paper and return to the oven for a further few minutes until just golden, then remove once again and using a pastry brush, paint the base with egg white. Pop back in the oven for literally 2–3 minutes until the surface is shiny and crisp.

For the filling, melt the chocolate in the usual way, beat in the cheese, crème fraîche and fruit zest. It will be quite sloppy so put in the fridge to firm up. Just before serving, spread this inside the pastry case and arrange the strawberries on top. Be generous with these – you don't want great white gaps showing through. Dust the top with sieved icing sugar and decorate with a couple of strawberry leaves and a flower.

Tip from the Sink ~

Don't be tempted to fill the tart too far in advance or the pastry may go soggy.

Ginger Semi-Freddo

It was Jonathan Young, Editor of The Field, *not only a gifted journalist and accomplished all-round sportsman, but also a dab hand at the stove, who taught me that the addition of a tin of condensed milk negates the need for endless churning in an ice cream maker and also prevents crystals from forming. A useful tip.*

SERVES 6–8

600 ml (1 pint) double cream

Jar stem ginger and its syrup

Tin of condensed milk

Small tub of crème fraîche

Splash Stone's ginger wine – optional

3 egg whites

Line a terrine tin with cling-film. Whip the cream to soft peaks, chop up the ginger into very fine slivers and mix in together with the syrup, condensed milk, ginger wine (if using) and crème fraîche. Whisk the egg whites until stiff and fold in with a metal spoon. Pour into the tin and place in the deep-freeze until just before serving.

Tip from the Sink ∼

Fill profiteroles with this and serve with chocolate sauce.

Rosie's Chocolate Ice Cream

RA and I enjoyed some wonderful holidays in South Africa. A visit to The Coach House, nestling in the foothills of the Drakensberg Mountains, was always our first stop. A haven of peace and beauty, it boasts some of this country's finest cooking. The puddings are all the work of the fabulous Rosie and it is this same smiling lady who wagons her trolley, groaning under a welter of sweet treats, adeptly and majestically round the dining room. Her ice creams, which come in at least six different flavours, are stored in miniature milk-churn style vessels designed to keep them cool. The chocolate is the best I have ever tasted.

SERVES 12

400 g (14 oz) dark chocolate, grated

2 teaspoons instant coffee
  granules/powder

2 tablespoons cocoa powder

3 tablespoons water

12 eggs, separated

200 g (7 oz) icing sugar

3 cups (750 ml) double cream

Melt half the chocolate with the coffee, cocoa and water then leave to cool. Beat the egg whites until stiff, gradually beat in the icing sugar until the mixture is thick and shiny. Beat the egg yolks until thick and mousse-like and fold into the egg whites. Whip the cream until it forms soft peaks and fold into the egg mixture, followed by the melted chocolate. Add the remaining chocolate and mix in carefully. Put into an ice cream maker and process for 25 minutes. If you do not have a machine, put in the freezer and when almost frozen, remove and beat well. Repeat this process twice.

Crème Brulée with Plums

The characteristics of this timeless classic may be altered with a whole host of different flavourings ranging from herbs such as rosemary, to flowers e.g. lavender as well as a plethora of fruits. The French even use chicory to produce that bitter coffee taste. When plums are in season, they lift the richness of this pudding pleasingly.

500 g (1 lb) finest plums	4 egg yolks
Pinch cinnamon powder	1 tablespoon caster sugar
300 ml (½ pint) double cream	Icing sugar
1 vanilla pod, split lengthways	

Preheat the oven to 160°C/325°F/gas mark 3. Poach the plums in a little water together with the cinnamon powder and some sugar if necessary until just soft then remove with a slotted spoon, leaving the cooking juices behind. Divide the fruit between four small ramekins. Put the cream and the vanilla pod into a pan and heat until scalding but do not let it burn. Beat the eggs and sugar together until pale and creamy then stir into the cream. Place in a bowl over a pan of simmering water and stir over a low heat until the custard coats the back of the spoon. Remove the vanilla pod and pour the cream over the plums in the ramekins. Stand in a bain-marie half filled with hot water and bake in the oven for 15 minutes until just set. Remove, leave until completely cool then refrigerate – preferably overnight.

For the brulée – dust the surfaces with icing sugar then place under a hot grill or burnish with a blow torch.

Tip from the Sink ～

Spritz the sugar toppings with a spray of water as this helps them brulée evenly.

Ginger Biscuit Pudding

I found this whilst looking through my very first recipe book. It's a real sweet-toothed blast from the past and though it could hardly be considered gourmet food by today's standards, it remains, for me, one of those reassuringly steadfast national treasures of the pudding department.

SERVES 8

4 packets ginger nuts

1 cup of strong black instant coffee

300 ml (½ pint) double cream

Stem ginger, chopped

Ginger marmalade or jam

Cointreau

Line a 1 litre (1¾ pint) capacity terrine tin with cling-film. Dunk the biscuits in the coffee and place a layer in the base of the tin. Whip the cream until stiff then mix in the marmalade, stem ginger and a tot or two of Cointreau. Spread over the biscuits then build up layers until all the ingredients have been used up. Refrigerate and slice to serve.

Sauces, Standbys and Sides

*T*HIS CHAPTER IS PROBABLY one of the most important in any cookbook since it contains all those little nuggets which do not necessarily fall into any one specific category but which are, nevertheless, so essential to good cuisine. It is something to dip into when searching for that touch of inspiration to breathe a bit of life into existing recipes and lift them out of the ordinary.

First, sauces. Frequently, a simply cooked piece of fish or meat can be elevated to new heights by a judiciously flavoured sauce. And, the great thing about most of these is that they can be prepared in advance. If I had to name one Desert Island Culinary Luxury (apart from an oyster knife!) then it would be my chicken stock, from which so many of my savoury sauces emanate. A good, concentrated stock of jellied consistency (most important this, as it removes the need to use flour to thicken) is the key to creating great sauces and I am never without a supply of it in the deep-freeze. Clean, plastic milk cartons with a screw lid are brilliant for storing it in.

As for standbys – we all need a ready, reliable supply of them up our sleeve for those spur-of-the-moment quick fixes when occasions demand lightning inspiration and time is short. Unpretentious, unmucked-about-with foods are, after all, the type of thing we all want to come back to – again and again.

Sides include various suggestions as to what to do with vegetables – either to sit happily alongside other ingredients or, indeed, as a course in their own right. In both instances, they will stand up well to being tinkered with, and adapted to suit your own personal tastes.

Sauces

My Chicken Stock

Take the cooked carcass of a chicken, break up the bones and throw into a roasting pan along with a couple of roughly chopped onions (leave skins on), and a few herbs. Drizzle over 3–4 tablespoons olive oil and put in a hot oven. This process increases the depth of flavour and colour of the stock. When nicely browned (approximately 20 minutes), remove from the oven and transfer to a large pan. Cover with cold water and add a few more vegetables – whatever is to hand: a stick of celery, carrot tops and tails, mushroom stalks or some leek trimmings. Herbs may also be used – a bay leaf, some parsley stalks or a few sprigs of thyme. Shake in a few black peppercorns and bring the liquid to the boil then reduce to a simmer and leave on the heat for at least 4–5 hours topping up with more water regularly, i.e. every time you pass the pan. You may think the liquid is simply evaporating and boiling away but what is actually happening is that what goes up in steam is merely the water and what remains in the pan is the concentration of true flavours. Remove from the stove, drain through a sieve and put the liquid into the fridge to solidify. Before use, remove the layer of fat with a slotted spoon and discard. If the liquid does not set to a rich jellied consistency, then you have not boiled it up for long enough and the sauces made from the liquid will not possess that coating quality which obviates the need for loathsome thickening agents.

N.B. If you do not have a carcass to hand, then ask your butcher for some chicken wings and proceed as above with these.

Tips from the Sink ~

- *Rosie Abel-Smith – garden designer extraordinaire as well as a superb cook – returns the bones to the pan once the stock has been drained off, refills it with water and covers with a lid then leaves it for a further 24 hours in the top left hand oven of a four-door Aga. Thereafter, she feeds the by now completely softened contents to her pack of dogs and says it keeps them going for days!*

- *The addition of a marrow bone (available from your butcher) will give extra depth of flavour to the stock – ideal when making consommé.*

Anchovy Butter

Sauces, Standbys and Sides

Do you remember when 'Grilled steak with Beurre Maître'd' was billed as the height of fashionable restaurant fare? I must confess that I do and whilst it has long since been usurped from pole position it nevertheless remains a constant 'must' in my fridge. I like to watch the solid blob placed on top of a piece of grilled meat begin to dissolve, then run, all over its surface as the heat melts it.

Anchovy butter packs a moreish punch, is great when used to make anchovy, as opposed to garlic, bread and I happen also to love it spread on toast or crumpets for a winter's day teatime treat. Furthermore, it turns that thoroughly overrated vegetable, broccoli, into something altogether far more exciting.

100 g (4 oz) butter
6 anchovy fillets, patted dry
1 teaspoon Gentleman's Relish if available

Simply pound together the butter and anchovy fillets with a pestle and mortar or whiz in the small bowl of a processor then beat in the Gentleman's Relish if using. Add more anchovies for a stronger flavour.

Jo's Bread Sauce

Jo Wood is a talented interior designer whose business spans a worldwide list of clients. She is also a great home-maker and an excellent cook – though how she finds the time for the latter I am never sure. Her bread sauce beats all others. I eat it straight from the spoon and never mind the other accoutrements!

Small onion	175 g (6 oz) white breadcrumbs
25 g (1 oz) butter	2 tablespoons cream
12–15 cloves	Seasoning and nutmeg
600 ml (1 pint) milk	

Cut the onion into one-third and two-thirds and finely chop the one-third then sweat it in a saucepan in half the butter without browning. Stud the remaining chunk of onion with cloves into the cut side, add to the pan together with three quarters of the milk. Bring to the boil and simmer gently for half an hour. Set aside and leave to stand for another half an hour.

Just before serving, remove the clove-studded onion and discard. Tip in the breadcrumbs and bring to the boil for 2–3 minutes, stirring continuously. Add the last bit of butter and cream, seasoning and nutmeg. Sip to taste!

Tip from the Sink ～

To make this ahead, gently pour a covering of milk over the back of a spoon onto the sauce and set aside. When required, stir in the milk and reheat.

Good Vinaigrette

I wouldn't go so far as to call this the ultimate vinaigrette – does such a single recipe exist I wonder? Nevertheless, this is a good basic method to which garlic, herbs and other flavourings may be added according to whim and fancy. Sometimes, to finish, I add a little hazel or walnut oil to give it another dimension or, in their absence, a pinch of curry powder. This keeps well and doesn't need to be stored in the fridge.

125 ml (4 fl oz) good olive oil
125 ml (4 fl oz) groundnut or sunflower oil
½ teaspoon Maldon sea salt, crushed
½ teaspoon Dijon mustard
Black/white peppercorns, freshly ground

Squeeze of lemon juice
1 tablespoon caster sugar – I often use Candarel instead
2 tablespoons white, red wine, sherry or balsamic vinegar

Mix the vinegar of your choice together with the olive and groundnut oils, the mustard, sugar and lemon juice. Season and store in a jar, shaking well before use.

Tip from the Sink ∼

Oils kept in a warm place or near the Aga will blend together more easily.

Mayonnaise

It is rumoured that if enough oil is added to a mere two egg yolks then you can end up with 90 litres (20 gallons) of mayonnaise. I wouldn't know as I've never tried it!

2 egg yolks	300 ml (½ pint) groundnut oil
½ teaspoon Dijon mustard	1 teaspoon lemon juice
Pinch sugar	Seasoning
1½ tablespoon white wine vinegar	1 tablespoon boiling water (optional)
300 ml (½ pint) lightish olive oil	

Put the egg yolks, sugar and mustard in a bowl and begin adding the olive oil slowly, one drop at a time, beating all the time with either a wire whisk or electric mixer so that the mixture begins to emulsify and thicken. Once this has been achieved, the process can be speeded up. Next, add the white wine vinegar followed by the remaining oil. Sharpen with the lemon juice as necessary then season. If the mayonnaise is very thick in consistency then mix in one tablespoon of boiling water. Cover and refrigerate.

Tips from the Sink ∼

- *Crushed cloves of garlic may be added to make an aioli which is delicious served with a plate of crudités. Herbs may also be added or some blanched watercress may be blended in to make a sauce for salmon.*

- *Should the mayonnaise curdle at any stage, add another egg yolk and proceed or beat in an ice cube.*

- *Mayonnaise in a dash? Simply whizz two whole eggs in a food-processor with the mustard and sugar and pour the oil through the funnel with the machine running. Finish as above.*

Get Ahead Hollandaise Sauce

This recipe comes from Richenda, who helps me with my cooking demos. I spent years making this in a somewhat laborious manner until, one day during a course, I gave this task to Richenda who proved to me that my method was far too long winded. She's quite right – naturally – and not only is her recipe, given to her by Mirabel Helme (another wonderful cook) far quicker but it is also reassuringly foolproof and can be made several hours in advance and left to stand somewhere warm.

3 egg yolks	1 tablespoon white wine vinegar
Pinch of caster sugar	Juice of ½ lemon
Seasoning	175 g (6 oz) butter

Put the egg yolks, sugar and seasoning into the bowl of a Magimix (or similar) and whiz together. Meanwhile heat the white wine vinegar and lemon juice in a pan until boiling then pour into the machine. In a separate pan, melt the butter until sizzling but not burning, then slowly pour into the egg mixture with the machine running until all is incorporated. The sauce is done.

Taste to check seasoning and adjust if necessary. Turn the mixture into a warmed bowl, cover and leave to stand on the side of the Aga or in a warm place (near the kettle) until ready to serve. Chopped fresh herbs may be added – the addition of mint makes this an excellent sauce to accompany lamb. Double cream will increase the quantity of sauce very effectively.

Sauce Bordelaise

As its name suggests, this is a red wine sauce which makes an extremely versatile accompaniment to a whole host of ingredients. I like to serve it with red meats, e.g. steak, offal such as kidneys and liver, as well as game. It is also a good match for fish – salmon, monkfish, hake and halibut – and also conveniently dispels the myth that only white wine should be drunk with fish.

2 shallots, peeled and finely diced	2 large tablespoons concentrated
1 garlic clove, peeled but not crushed	chicken stock
Sprig of thyme	50 g (2 oz) cold butter, cubed
2 glasses red wine	Splash of port or Ribena

Put the shallots, garlic and thyme into a saucepan and pour in the red wine then reduce to 2 tablespoons. Add the chicken stock and reduce again to a sauce-like consistency. Whisk in the butter and a drop more red wine, plus the port or Ribena to enhance the flavour. Season, strain and reheat to serve.

Tip from the Sink ~

The addition of a couple of squares of dark chocolate, high in cocoa content, give it extra richness which makes it the perfect partner for venison dishes.

Caraffini Sauce

This comes from my favourite Italian restaurant in London. They serve it here with their carpaccio.

200 ml (6½ fl oz) tub crème fraîche	Juice ½ lemon
200 ml (6½ fl oz) home-made mayonnaise	1 teaspoon horseradish
1 teaspoon (or more) Dijon mustard	Seasoning

Simply mix all the ingredients together.

Pesto Sauce

To me, this IS summer in a jar and it is a handy thing to have in the fridge. I make mine omitting the Parmesan cheese though I might grate this over separately if serving with pasta. I also prefer it without garlic. Pesto is also ideal as a dressing for fish, tricolore salad (if too thick run it down with some olive oil) as well as for drizzling over the tops of tomato tartlets. It's also good with griddled aubergines as well as with lamb. Just one word of warning – basil leaves bruise easily so take care when chopping them – it's best to tear them by hand, and don't over process otherwise they will end up tasting bitter.

50 g (2 oz) basil leaves, stems removed and finely chopped	50 g (2 oz) pine nuts, lightly toasted
6 tablespoons extra virgin olive oil	Salt

Blend to a smooth consistency or else pound together in a pestle and mortar.

Tip from the Sink ~

Try replacing the basil with flat leaf parsley leaves and use this as a garnish for soups or stir a teaspoon or two through some fresh white crab meat.

Chocolate Sauce

Great to have up one's sleeve. It will cheer up even the most mundane of puddings and is delicious with ice cream-filled profiteroles and unbeatable when slaked over poached pears.

175 g (6 oz) dark chocolate, minimum 75% cocoa content	175 g (6 oz) butter Squirt of golden syrup

Break the chocolate into squares and put in a bowl together with the butter. Leave to stand on the side of the Aga until melted or stand the bowl over a saucepan of simmering, not boiling, water – making sure the base does not touch the water. Stir until melted and completely smooth then add the golden syrup.

Raspberry Sauce

I have an aversion to the word 'coulis'. It conjures up visions of pretentious restaurant-speak language. Usually the sort of poncy place where all the food arrives in 'stacks': the meat and fish is to be found sitting on beds – or worse still – pillows of herb-scented vegetables flavoured with an aromatic jus... bla, bla and, likewise, their puddings tend to come with a coulis of ... No! In essence, this is a simple sauce, without frills and tastes great just as it is. You can also make it with strawberries – whichever are to hand, really. For high days and holidays, this can be jazzed up with a little kirsch or Eau de Vie de Framboise *or* Fraise *liqueur.*

350 g (12 oz) raspberries – frozen are fine
2 tablespoons brown sugar
Juice of a lemon

Put the ingredients into a saucepan and heat through until just bubbling then sieve. If it is too thick, thin down with a little warm water.

Tip from the Sink ∼

When sieving this, one labour-saving device is to push the purée through using the back of a ladle rather than an ordinary spoon. Much quicker.

Sauce Poivrade

This recipe was given to me by the chef at Wiltons, that Jermyn Street Restaurant in the Capital, famed since 1742 for its finest oysters, fish and game. The quantities are unspecified rather, I imagine, because it would be made up and used in greater quantities than you and I might require at home. It's a punchy sauce and the perfect match with hare or venison which have been marinated in the following. Red wine, chopped onions, carrots, leeks, celery, a bay leaf, stick of cinnamon, some parsley stalks and around a dozen bruised juniper berries all put in a saucepan and simmered for around 15 minutes then left to cool before covering the meat.

For the Sauce	Crushed white peppercorns
The above marinade	Redcurrant jelly
Red wine	Good game or chicken stock
Chopped onion	Cold butter

Put the marinade plus the red wine, chopped onion and crushed white peppercorns into a pan and reduce down slowly by at least two-thirds then add the redcurrant jelly and the stock and allow to cook down for a further 45 minutes. Season and pass through a fine sieve then whisk in a few cubes of cold butter before serving.

Salsa Verde

An ace accompaniment to grilled chicken, fish and to go with pasta dishes, vegetables and salads. Just about anything, in fact.

2 tablespoons each roughly chopped flat leaf parsley and mint leaves	1 clove garlic
3 tablespoons capers, drained and rinsed	1 teaspoon Dijon mustard
Small tin anchovy fillets, drained	1–1½ tablespoons lemon juice
	125 ml (4 fl oz) extra virgin olive oil

Pile the parsley, mint, capers, anchovies and garlic onto a chopping board and grind to a coarse paste, or do so using a pestle and mortar. If using a board, transfer these ingredients to a bowl then stir in the lemon juice, mustard, olive oil and, if you wish, a smidgeon of sea salt.

Standbys

Lemon Curd

What can possibly beat a jar of home-made curd – be it Jaffa orange, lime, raspberry or this lemon version? It is eaten with crumpets or on toast and is also a wonderful filling for cakes and a worthy substitute to the ubiquitous layer of jam in Queen of Puddings.

2 lemons, juice and zest
100 g (4 oz) unsalted butter, cut into small cubes

3 eggs
225 g (8 oz) caster sugar

Put the lemon zest and the juice into a bowl set over a pan of simmering water. Add the rest of the ingredients, and stir until the butter has melted and the sugar dissolved. Cook slowly until the mixture thickens. Allow to cool then pour into a clean jar and store in the fridge.

Seville Marmalade

These oranges usually appear in the shops around mid January. I never bother freezing them to use at a later date – way too bulky. Instead, dust down the preserving pan, roll up your sleeves, turn on the iPod and become a Marmalade Queen for a day. And don't restrict this delicious conserve purely to the breakfast table. I know of one chef who religiously adds it to stews, and it is also very good in puddings and cakes as well as a glaze for meats and, additionally, it can be used to sauce duck, especially wild mallard – and never mind the quips about 'duck à l'orange'!

1½ kg (3 lbs) Seville oranges	2 litres (3½ pints) water
Juice of 2 lemons	2 very generous dollops of black
3 kg (6 lbs) sugar	treacle

Warm the sugar in a bowl or pan. (I stand mine on the side of the Aga.)

Put the whole oranges and lemon juice into another pan and cover with the water and weight (a slightly too small lid or a circular tin tray will do the trick). Bring to the boil, remove the makeshift weights and cover with a fitting lid and put in the simmering oven of the Aga if you have one (or else cook very gently on top of the stove) until the fruit is completely soft. Remove the fruit, leave until cool enough to handle then cut in half, scoop out the pips and pith and return to the liquid. Bring to the boil for 6 minutes and strain. Pour half this liquid into a saucepan. Slice up the peel and add half the quantity to the pan plus half the sugar and half the treacle. Stir to dissolve then boil for at least 20 minutes until setting point is reached. Repeat for a second batch and then transfer to sterilised jars. Seal and label.

Tip from the Sink ~

Don't worry unduly if the marmalade is reluctant to reach setting point which, just sometimes, it refuses point-blank to do. Instead, console yourself with the fact that, the runnier it is, the further it will go!

Cheese Sables

The perfect prelunch (or supper) nibble, these also make a popular present for a friend. Simply fill a jar with them and tie a ribbon around the lid. This recipe comes from The Coach House where Chipps Mann runs all manner of lovely courses.

100 g (4 oz) grated cheese e.g. mature Cheddar, Parmesan, Emmental etc.	4 teaspoons plain flour

Preheat the oven to 190°C/375°F/gas mark 5. Simply put the cheese(s) and flour into a bowl and mix by hand. Press blobs onto a baking tray lined with Bake-o-Glide and cook until golden brown, approximately 3–4 minutes.

Gougere Puffs

Choux puffs make ideal appetisers. In Burgundy they are often served at wine tastings, straight from the oven. I sometimes offer them with soup.

100 g (4 oz) butter	85 g (3½ oz) plain flour, sifted
Pinch of sea salt	4 eggs, beaten
250 ml (8 fl oz) cold water	50 g (2 oz) grated Gruyère cheese

Preheat the oven to 190°C/375°F/gas mark 5. Combine the butter, salt and water in a heavy-based saucepan and bring to the boil, whisking occasionally. Once the mixture boils, remove from the heat immediately and add the flour then beat vigorously until the mixture comes away from the sides of the pan. Return to a low heat and continue beating for a minute to dry out the dough. Next, add the eggs gradually and beat in after each one then, finally, the cheese which will melt in the heat. Spoon heaped teaspoonfuls onto a baking sheet – make sure they are well spaced out – either lined with greaseproof paper or a sheet of Bake-o-Glide, then cook in the oven for approximately 15–20 minutes until puffed up and an even golden brown. Transfer to a rack to cool slightly then serve.

Tip from the Sink ⁓

Omit the cheese from the mixture and replace with a tablespoon of caster sugar. Cook as above then leave to cool before filling with ice cream and pouring on the chocolate sauce for a heavenly pudding.

Eggy Bread

Great with crisply grilled bacon rashers, this vanishes as fast as it is made.

3 eggs	Seasoning
Dash of milk	Butter
Thickish slices white bread cut from a loaf	

Beat the eggs in a bowl together with the milk, then season. Transfer to a flat dish and dip the bread into the mixture so it is sodden on both sides. Heat a generous nut of butter in a frying pan and, when foaming, add the bread and cook on first one side then the other so it is deliciously crisp and golden.

Sportsman's Special

Sally Ewart, who lives up in the Borders, kindly gave me this recipe. It's as well known in certain sporting circles as some of those die-hard flask fillers such as Percy Specials and makes a wonderfully heart-warming high tea-style treat to come home to. After a long day outdoors it will assuage the hungriest of appetites though Sally assures me that any leftovers are great used as a cold filling for sandwiches. I have to admit that whenever I have been anywhere near it, the dish has always been scraped clean! If you can wait long enough, it's also excellent for supper and can be left ready ahead just to heat through at the last minute.

175 g (6 oz) shelled prawns, drained on kitchen paper

8 rashers back bacon, cooked until crisp then roughly chopped

175 g (6 oz) ham, diced

6 eggs, (lightly) hard- boiled

600 ml (1 pint)+ of béchamel sauce, flavoured with plenty of strong Cheddar cheese – or use Beaufort – well seasoned

4 tomatoes, thinly sliced

4 slices white bread, buttered and cut into triangles

Preheat the oven to 180°C/350°F/gas mark 4. Dot the eggs over the base of a large oven-proof dish (this is not something to be made in small quantities!) followed by the ham, prawns and bacon, then cover with the sauce. Cover the surface with rows of tomato rings alternated with overlapping slices of bread. Bake in the oven for around 20 minutes until the top is golden and bubbling brown, and the bread has toasted nicely.

Soda Bread

I've never indulged very much in bread-baking sessions probably because one of the few cooking lessons I've ever had involved an entire morning spent making croissants for at least 75 people. I found this, along with the time required to allow yeast-based breads to prove and rise, all rather too time-consuming for my liking. Cakes of soda bread, on the other hand, are an entirely different matter and there's something rather smug-making about knocking out one of these in a matter of minutes and bringing it still warm to the table. Its rough-hewn appearance bears ample testimony to the fact it really is home-made. Slice it, then slather with the finest butter or, better still, enjoy it with potted shrimps!

275 g (10 oz) stoneground wholemeal flour
275 g (10 oz) plain white flour
1 teaspoon bicarbonate of soda

1 tablespoon black treacle
1 teaspoon salt
450 ml (16 fl oz) buttermilk

Preheat the oven to 190°C/375°F/gas mark 5. Put the two types of flour into a large bowl, make a well in the centre and pour in the buttermilk. Add the bicarbonate of soda, treacle and salt and mix together using your hands. Turn out onto a lightly floured surface and lightly knead it then pat into a round shape. Put a deep cross in the top and bake in the oven for around 40–45 minutes or until it sounds hollow when the base is tapped.

M's Lemon Drizzle Cake

Nothing beats sneaking into the larder, snatching the lid off an ancient and battered painted tin to find a freshly baked cake nestling inside. There was always one at home for tea and this particular one I associate with my mother – an extremely good baker.

150 g (5 oz) self-raising flour
100 g (4 oz) caster sugar
100 g (4 oz) soft butter
2 eggs
2 tablespoons lemon curd

Grated zest of ½ lemon

For the Glaze
Grated zest and juice of ½ lemon
1 dessertspoon caster sugar

Preheat the oven to 190°C/375°F/gas mark 5. Whizz all the cake ingredients together and turn into a 15–18 cm (6–7 inch) cake tin, lined with greaseproof paper and bake for approximately 50 minutes until golden brown and firm to the touch.

Whilst it is cooling, melt the sugar in a pan together with the lemon juice and zest. Prick the cake all over and pour on. Remove the sponge from the tin once completely cold.

Orange Easter Biscuits

I once ate a whole tin of these in one sitting but even such a binge failed to cure me of my addiction to them. If, unlike me, you can restrain yourself they are also very good alongside ice creams and fruit fools.

225 g (8 oz) soft butter
175 g (6 oz) caster sugar
3 egg yolks

Grated zest of an orange
375 g (13 oz) plain flour
50 g (2 oz) currants

Cream the butter and sugar together until light and fluffy then beat in the egg yolks and orange zest then fold in the flour. Add the currants and knead to a smooth dough. Wrap in cling-film and chill in the fridge for half an hour before rolling out on a lightly floured surface. Press out rounds using a fluted cutter, transfer to a lightly greased baking tray and cook in the oven for 15–20 minutes until very lightly coloured. Transfer to a wire cooling rack and sprinkle immediately with caster sugar.

Janet's Flapjacks

Janet does all the food for shooting lunches at Salperton Park Estate. There is no possible danger of Guns ever going hungry. Her fruitcake and chocolate brownies are the business. And her only rival when it comes to her flapjacks is Mandy Woolliams. Both agree that their success lies in making them using a cheap brand of porridge oats (the smaller the flakes the better they stick together) and to undercook them.

100 g (4 oz) butter	1 tablespoon golden syrup
100 g (4 oz) soft brown sugar	175 g (6 oz) porridge oats

Preheat the oven to 140°C/275°F/gas mark 1. Melt the butter, sugar and syrup. Stir in the oats and put into a lined tin. Bake for approximately 12–15 minutes (but watch them!) until the mixture begins to bubble in the middle. Remove and leave to cool before cutting up.

Tip from the Sink ~

Try adding grated apple and a little cinnamon to these or some pecan nut pieces.

Savouries

So English a dish, so seldom seen nowadays. Perhaps partly because they generally require last minute attention which is not ideal for the single-handed host/cook. I never fail to notice, however, that a savoury is always greeted with huge enthusiasm, particularly amongst beef-eating males. No wonder, then, that they have remained firmly on the menus at so many Gentlemen's Dining Clubs and long-established restaurants. Elsewhere they are more likely to be presented as a canapé – think devils-on-horseback, miniature Welsh Rarebit and Scotch Woodcock along with the preprandial drinks – but the following two suggestions can both be prepped in advance then simply slid under the grill at the very last minute and thus make a welcome return at the dinner table itself.

Stilton and Strawberry Jam Toasts

1 medium slice white bread per person	Stilton cheese
Good quality strawberry jam	

Toast the slices of bread on one side, cut off the crusts and spread the untoasted side with the jam then top with thin slices of cheese. Grill until bubbling.

Cheesey Wafers

Quicker by far than cheese straws – these are easy-peasy to rustle up.

Ice cream wafers
Mature cheddar cheese – finely grated

Press plenty of cheese down onto wafers then grill until lightly browned. Allow several of these per person, they slip down a real treat.

Sauces, Standbys and Sides

Liquid Standbys

Nella's Lemon Drink

Nella Matson always produces this after-dinner quencher for the girls (whilst the men are getting stuck into her husband's port). Knowing that they are the ones most likely to have drawn the short straw when it comes to driving home, this is a welcome aid to ward off the breathalyser.

1 large lemon, washed and quartered
6 ice cubes

2 tablespoons granulated sugar
750 ml (1¼ pints) cold water

Place the lemon in the processor and blitz with the other ingredients for 10 seconds only. (Any longer and it will develop a pithy taste.) Strain and serve in a large jug to which lemon slices, ice and mint may be added.

Elderflower Cordial

I have always been a great believer in living off the land and there is something so satisfying about gathering free foods. Somehow, the added thrill of not having to pay for these automatically makes them taste better! Don't forget also to scour the hedgerows (but only those well away from the roadside) throughout the year for nuts, nettles, berries and, of course, lace-capped fragrant elderflowers.

1 kg (2 lbs) granulated sugar, preferably unrefined
50 g (2 oz) citric acid or Vitamin C powder
5 lemons

20 heads elderflowers, shaken to remove any lingering bugs and insects
1 litre (1¾ pints) boiling water

Before you can make this, it will necessitate a trip to the local chemist. Don't be surprised if they ask you for what purpose you wish to purchase the citric acid or vitamin C powder. Apparently, it looks just like heroin! Once you have passed the pharmacist's interrogation … proceed.

Tip the sugar and citric acid into a large pan, halve the lemons and squeeze the juice into it, then add the shells and the elderflowers. Pour on the boiling water and place on the stove. Once the mixture has returned to the boil, cook for a couple of minutes then remove, cover and leave to stand overnight before straining and bottling. Keep in the fridge and dilute with water.

Tip from the Sink ⁓

Try adding a couple of tablespoons of this (undiluted) to gooseberry tarts and fools.

Bloody Mary

My first job in London was working at The Jockey Club for the Racecourse Association. If I am honest, I think my efforts in learning how to mix this excellent Sunday morning cocktail, which we made on a daily basis, took priority over any other part of my duties. You can use ordinary tomato juice though I find this a bit gloopy and prefer to use Clamato (always keep a supply in the fridge) which produces a Bloody Mary of rare authority. So good, some say, it barely needs the vodka to kick start it. Spice it up according to personal taste.

For a Large Jug

3–4 200 ml (6½ fl oz) bottles Clamato juice – available in good supermarkets, delis and individual wine merchants

Juice of at least one lemon

Worcester sauce

Few shakes Tabasco

Large teaspoon horseradish sauce

Celery salt

Tot (or two) of sherry

Measure(s) of vodka

Plenty of ice

Stick of celery

Pour the Clamato juice into the jug then add the lemon, sauces, celery salt and finally pour on the alcohol. Top with ice cubes, stir around well with the celery stalk and serve.

Sides

Tian of Aubergine, Spinach and Tomato

Shaun Hill kindly gave me this recipe. These are excellent alongside a dish of lamb and can be prepped ahead then reheated.

1 large aubergine	½ glass white wine
1 kg (2 lbs) tomatoes	Bay leaf
4 shallots	Sprig of thyme
2 cloves garlic	450 g (1 lb) young spinach, washed
2 tablespoons olive oil	25 g (1 oz) butter

Slice the aubergine into 4 rounds each about 1 cm (½ inch) thick then fry in 1 tablespoon of hot olive oil. Drain on kitchen paper. Next, skin and deseed the tomatoes. Chop the shallots and garlic very finely and fry without colouring in the remaining olive oil. Add the white wine, tomatoes and herbs and transfer the pan to a low oven and cook until dry then remove herbs.

Heat the butter in a pan and add the spinach. Season well and cook for 2–3 minutes until soft and wilted. Drain well pressing out all excess liquid.

To assemble, stand four stainless steel rings on a sheet of greaseproof paper, some butter wrappers or a piece of Bake-o-Glide then fill with the spinach followed by the tomato and top with the aubergine. Cover and reheat gently in the oven until warmed through.

Tip from the Sink ∼

Serve these as a starter accompanied by a tomato sauce or add a piece of goats' cheese to the top of each one and slide under a hot grill until well browned.

Petit Pois à la Dashers

This is my own version, less long-winded than the authentic recipe in that it omits the baby onions and shredded lettuce but is, nevertheless, still very good. The secret is in remembering to thaw out the peas before you come to cook them. Once you have eaten them in this way, you will never again boil them in water!

375–400 g (13–14 oz) petit pois, removed from freezer beforehand

1 teaspoon caster sugar

Packet of bacon lardons

Olive oil

Start by frying off the bacon in a frying pan until crisp then remove and set to one side. Add a slick of olive oil to the pan and then the peas with the sugar and cook for approximately 5–7 minutes until just done, stirring regularly. Return the lardons to the pan to warm through then serve.

Pickled Cucumber

So many people claim cucumber gives them indigestion. Prepared in this way, the salt disgorges the juices which cause this. I like to serve it alongside a timbale of fresh crab – its slight sharpness makes a perfect foil for the richness of the meat. Its also good prepared in this way then mixed with some crème fraîche and pepper to eat as a side salad.

1 cucumber, peeled and very thinly sliced – use a mandoline if you have one otherwise a sharp knife

Splash or two of white wine vinegar

Pinch of caster sugar

Dill leaves

Sea salt

Arrange the cucumber slices in a shallow dish, add the vinegar, sugar, salt and dill then weight down and leave to stand for at least 30 minutes. Remove from the liquid and serve.

Oven-Roasted Beetroot

Providing the beetroot is well washed and its whiskery parts have been removed, I never bother to peel it. This method of cooking enhances its sweet earthiness beautifully.

1 bunch beets, trimmed and washed

2 tablespoons olive oil

2 cloves garlic, peeled and thinly sliced

Shake or two balsamic vinegar

Small handful marjoram or thyme sprigs

Scattering sea salt

Preheat the oven to 190°C/375°F/gas mark 5. Chop the beetroot into chunks then lay on a very large double sheet of foil (you want to be able to fold this up to make a parcel) inside a baking tray. Add the oil, vinegar, garlic, herbs and sea salt then seal loosely and bake in the oven for at least an hour or until tender.

Tip from the Sink ～

A great veggie to serve with beef, game, a Sunday roast, smoked fish such as eel and also in salads with goats' cheese.

Trix with Tatties

Cheap, easily available, hugely adaptable – along with lemons, eggs, and onions – the modest potato is one of the most basic yet loveable ingredients known to any kitchen. Whether boiled, roasted, chipped, gratinéed, mashed, creamed with parsley purée or used as a thickening agent – life without the potato is unthinkable.

Potato, Rocket and Fresh Truffles

If Syndey Smith's idea of heaven was eating foie gras to the sound of trumpets then mine is in this Jewel in the Crown dish. But first, find your truffle, the holy grail of every gourmet ... I was once lucky enough to be sent by Country Life to Norcia in Italy to write about these buried treasures. Returning home laden with my own supply cast the traditional duty-free offerings into insignificance and for a week thereafter these miraculous tubers enhanced and embellished the flavour of every dish I ate.

Plenty of washed and dried rocket leaves	Extra virgin olive oil
450 g (1 lb) small waxy potatoes, such as Rattes de Touquet, cooked	Finest sea salt
	Fresh truffle and a truffle slicer

Arrange the rocket on plates, add the warm sliced potatoes, pour on the olive oil, scatter over sea salt and adorn the surface liberally with slivers of truffle.

Tip from the Sink ～

Try burying truffles in a jar of rice or amongst the eggs – both will absorb their unique scent and 'truffle' the resultant dishes.

Baked Potatoes with Snails

A baked potato is one of the most comforting foods on this planet... Once it's in the oven, preferably with a metal skewer speared through its middle (I've exploded many a baked spud over the years, and its presence will also help conduct heat hence it cooks more quickly) – there's nothing further to do except leave it for an hour or so, remove from the heat, don the oven gloves and ease out said skewer, slice off the top and push some cold butter inside. For something with a Gallic influence, though, try the following which originates from Christian Germain. A brilliant winter's night supper served with a crisp green salad, some warm crusty bread and a bottle of gutsy red wine!

4 medium sized floury potatoes, Maris Piper or King Edward
75 g (3 oz) butter
2 cloves garlic, crushed
½ cup double cream

3 tablespoons chopped parsley
200 g (7 oz) tin snails

Bake the potatoes in the usual way then slice in half, removing the flesh and mash well in a bowl. In a small pan, heat the butter, add the garlic and cook to soften for a few minutes. Pour in the cream, followed by the parsley and snails (drained of any liquid). Mix into the potato, check seasoning and pile back into the skins. Return to the oven just to heat through.

Sauces, Standbys and Sides

Small Sauté Potatoes in Goose Fat

Quicker than roasting spuds, I often turn to these. The point about goose fat is that it heats up to a far higher temperature than ordinary oil or butter so produces a really crisp potato with a fluffy interior. Simply lightly par boil some peeled potatoes – being careful not to leave them for too long. They still need to be pretty firm. Drain and leave to cool then dice into small, neat squares. Heat 3–4 tablespoons goose fat in a baking tin and when sizzling, add the potatoes along with some sea salt and rosemary. Roast until golden brown and crunchy.

Butternut and Carrot Purée with Star Anise

If you don't like the flavour of aniseed then omit the star anise. This makes a good vegetable to serve with both meat and game as well as with seared prawns or you can change direction halfway through and run it down with stock and a little crème fraîche to make a delicious soup.

1 whole butternut, peeled and seeded, cut into chunks
450 g (1 lb) carrots, peeled and chopped
2 star anise
Few sprigs tarragon and chopped leaves

2–3 tablespoons stock, either chicken or vegetable
1 tablespoon soft brown sugar
Seasoning

Put the butternut and carrots into a saucepan, add the stock, star anise, tarragon and sugar and cook, covered with a lid, until completely soft. Remove the star anise and tarragon sprigs and blend the other ingredients, plus some chopped tarragon leaves, to a smooth purée then check seasoning. If making in advance, reheat before serving.

Tip from the Sink ~

Err on the side of caution when adding liquid to cook these vegetables – too much and you will end up with a watery purée.

Picnics, Déjeuner sur l'herbe and Alfresco Dining

$\mathcal{P}$ICNICS EVOKE WAVES OF nostalgia in all of us. Days when the sun shone endlessly, skies were cloudless and beaches deserted are cherished memories. We tend to forget those numberless occasions we have all endured huddled round the tailgate of the car as the wind and rain lashed relentlessly down and fingers froze. No one ever said we British are not stoic and, despite such vagaries in the weather, the attractions of picnicking remain wonderfully undiminished and mercifully, a certain optimism prevails.

My own picnicking experiences can, at the very least, be described as varied. These range through the whole spectrum from the idyllic and memorably romantic and spiral downwards to the plainly catastrophic when disaster has struck. If and when those carefully laid plans do not progress as anticipated, a good dollop of humour is essential. Sometimes, it is the guest from hell who plays havoc with the proceedings. Take the bibulous participant who makes off with the drinks leaving the rest of the party gasping in Gobi Desert-like conditions; or the hazards of nature wreaking her revenge when the searing sun frazzles the dainty little cucumber sandwiches to something resembling cardboard, 'cooks on' the once perfect pink fillet of beef and then heats the bowl of mayonnaise to such a degree that it emerges with a sickening oil slick swimming on its surface. And as for bugs, beasts and insects, watch out for an army of ants who will invade any foods left carefully covered on the ground in the shade. Still, as the celebrated cookery writer Jane Grigson sagely observed, the success of any picnic depends on disaster.

The real heart of foolproof picnicking lies in simplicity whilst balancing this with a measure of elegance. A few basics are essential – plenty of napkins, a waterproof rug or two, cool boxes or bags, a corkscrew, bag for the rubbish and a damp cloth. Too much kit and it all becomes a travelling circus and the whole point and pleasure of picnicking is entirely lost. Leaving aside such exhausting formalities do yourself a favour and keep the presence of plastic or Tupperware and paper plates along with disposable cutlery to a minimum. A surfeit of these does tend to instantly downgrade the show!

Food which can be eaten in the fingers, with the help of a sharp knife or, at most, the sharing of a few communal forks, is the best sort to pack. Seasoned picnic givers will know to organise things in such a way that people can help themselves otherwise, as host, you will find yourself handing out plate after plate, glass after glass all day long. All too much of a palaver! And in this respect, the French have got it honed to perfection even if they have, rather irritatingly, even borrowed our word for this form of eating! For them, it's little more than a case of bon marché. Good crusty bread, some herb-infused olives, a bowl of crunchy radishes, a chunk of rough country-style pâté, a selection of salami, saucisson and cold meats along with a few other treats from the *traiteur* or charcuterie plus the perfect cheese at the exact point of oozing ripeness, white-blush peaches, a basket of cherries and some well-chilled wine.

But I like to think we are not such slouches ourselves. Cocktail sausages baked in honey or maple syrup and smeared with mustard; a basket of peeled quails' eggs to dip in celery salt and small squares of Pissaladière will kick-start the proceedings with élan. Then, to follow, a rich succulent hand-raised hot water crust pastry pie; a baked ham, glistening with a marmalade, honey and brown sugar glaze and carved to order; a smoked chicken whose flesh can be torn from the carcass and dipped into some guacamole or slices of smoked duck to plunge into damson chutney. Alongside, there might be small new potatoes dressed in vinaigrette and chives whilst still hot, wedges of tortilla or frittata and a cherry tomato, broad bean and basil salad with baby gem lettuce leaves to use as a scoop. A hunk of gorgonzola with stalks of celery to spoon it up, ripe nectarines plus a tin of squidgy chocolate brownies will all go down a storm and surely make a worthy feast this side of the Channel.

As far as *déjeuner sur l'herbe* and alfresco dining are concerned, our predecessors have been enjoying this since time immemorial though it must be said, this was usually done with great pomp and ceremony in gazebos and pavilions expertly built for this purpose. In those days, the entire contents of the dining room would be transported to such venues and the participants would be lavishly served and waited upon by a retinue of uniformed staff. Nowadays, however, eating alfresco very often involves a last minute decision when the weather has taken an unexpected turn for the better. Suddenly, there is a sprint for the garden furniture which is dragged out of its winter hibernation and hastily wiped down. Perhaps it is the primal instinct within us that unerringly makes eating out of doors feel so right, so agreeable and so delightfully celebratory. Once again, the food needs to be straightforward and devoid of frills though, given it may only have to be transported a matter of a few yards from the kitchen, there are fewer constrictions when it comes to what is suitable. I am no great Barbecue Queen, preferring to leave that task to someone more competent and, after all, most men consider it is their domain; though do avoid, if possible, those ardent pyrotechnics! Properly done, minus the hazards of billowing fires, flames and smokescreens, there is nothing nicer though than open-air grilled foods with garlic and herbs from the garden or, even better – for really large numbers – a whole roasted sheep or pig on a spit. Anything goes when dining alfresco, just so long as it doesn't involve flaccid poached salmon, gloopy Coronation chicken and sad summer pudding resembling a collapsed sand castle. Perhaps some bruschetta to start or just plain tapenade spread on toasted French bread, then gravadlax or salmon ceviche served with crème fraîche and chives, tomato and red onion salad, egg and smoked haddock mousse and a plate of oven roast vegetables with aioli and a glazed fruit tart to finish – all are perfect for enjoying in the open air.

The recipes offered in this chapter offer infinite possibilities for each and every style of outdoor eating, so mix and match as befits the occasion, the weather and the situation.

Tortilla

This thick egg-cake is a faithful friend; reliable and solid – in most senses! My version though tends to vary according to what is in the fridge and store cupboard. Leftover ham, chicken or cold sausages, neatly chopped, may also be included.

6 eggs	100 g (4 oz) grated cheese, Parmesan or
Seasoning	mature Cheddar
Dash of milk	100 g (4 oz) petit pois, cooked
2 tablespoons flat leaf parsley, leaves only,	4–6 rashers back bacon, cooked until crisp
scissored	then roughly chopped
Small tin of sweetcorn, drained	

Beat the eggs in a bowl with a fork, adding the milk and plenty of seasoning. Mix in all the remaining ingredients. Melt a nut of butter in a large non-stick frying pan and, when foaming, pour everything in. Cook over a gentle heat for at least 30 minutes, tipping the pan from time to time so that the liquid runs down to the base of the pan and cooks, until set. Remove and leave until completely cold.

Omelette Terrine

This involves a bit more work but the end result is superb. It also makes an elegant first course for a supper or dinner party. Before you start, match the width of the frying pan, which must be non-stick, to the length of the terrine tin to ensure a neat fit! Make it a day ahead so it has time to 'set' properly in the tin which will make it easier to slice.

12 eggs
Seasoning
Butter

Fillings
100 g (4 oz) spinach, blanched,
    drained and squeezed dry

100 g (4 oz) grated cheese and 3 hard-
    boiled eggs, cut into slivers
Jar of sun-dried tomatoes, drained,
    dried and roughly chopped then
    mixed with chopped basil
Seasoning

Line the terrine tin with cling-film, making sure there is a generous overhang. In three individual mixing bowls, beat 4 eggs into each one and season. Heat the frying pan with a nut of butter and when foaming, pour in the eggs from the first bowl and cook as for a normal omelette, adding the first filling. When ready, fold over into three and slide into the tin lengthways. Cook the remaining two omelettes and place on top of one another in the tin. When completed, cover with the cling-film, lightly weight and refrigerate over-night. Be careful not to use anything too heavy as it will simply press all the liquid out of each omelette. To serve, turn out onto a board and cut into tranches.

Tip from the Sink ~

Serve it with vinaigrette to which some scissored herbs and sun-dried tomatoes have been added.

Cucumber and Mint Soup

Think Mediterranean tadzeki – most commonly served alongside dishes such as roast lamb or, in the case of cucumber raita to which it is closely related, as a cooling contrast to hot Indian curries. Here I have simply run it down with milk to make a light summer soup.

2 cucumbers, peeled and seeded and roughly chopped	Seasoning
300 ml (10 fl oz) plain Greek yoghurt	Juice of small lemon
Large handful mint leaves, chopped	300 ml (½ pint) milk

Simply process all the ingredients together then refrigerate until required.

Smoked Mackerel Pâté

Real fast food, this one is child's play!

2–3 smoked mackerel fillets, skinned	1 teaspoon horseradish sauce
200 g (7 oz) tub of cream cheese	Juice of ½ lemon
200 g (7 oz) tub crème fraîche	Pepper

Simply blitz all the ingredients together until smooth.

Tip from the Sink ∼

To make this into a dip, slacken the mixture with some single cream.

Salmon with Pesto and Parma Ham

These are a breeze to rustle up.

4 salmon fillets, skinned and checked for
any pinbones

Small jar of pesto
4 slices of Parma ham

Preheat the oven to 180°C/350°F/gas mark 4. Simply smear some pesto over the top side of each piece of salmon and then wrap in a sheet of Parma ham. Place on a baking sheet and put in the oven for around 12 minutes just until the ham has started to brown and the parcels are sizzling. Serve either hot or cold.

Chicken Thighs with Herbs and Sea Salt

There's nothing elaborate about this. It's just plain and perfect finger food, and meaty thighs, with their flavoursome dark meat, respond well to barbecuing and grilling. During summer months, I raid the potager, well – given my limited gardening skills – those belonging to green fingered friends, and pick marjoram, different flavoured thyme sprigs, rosemary, parsley, mint and sage which I tie up in great bunches and hang above the Aga. Once dried (this takes a few days), strip the leaves from the stalks and pound in the processor together with some furls of dried lemon zest then store in a jar. Scattered over meats and poultry they are far superior to the aged pot of Herbes de Provence which were brought back from France years ago and have languished since then in the back of the cupboard, turning to musty dust!

8 chicken thighs, skin on
2–3 tablespoons herbs (see above)

Generous scattering of sea salt
3–4 tablespoons olive oil

Simply cut slashes in the skin of the meat and marinate in the herbs, oil and salt for several hours then cook under a hot grill (if you don't have one then use a griddle pan on the stove) turning regularly until cooked through. Finish with a squeeze of lemon juice.

Potato Pie

A dish of potatoes enhances any occasion. Whether boiled new potatoes wrapped in Parma ham, roasted then served alongside an avocado dip or tossed whilst still hot in vinaigrette and liberally scattered with snipped chives; or a wickedly rich Gratin Dauphinois, to be eaten either hot or cold, as well as this less familiar pie.

SERVES 8

350 g (12 oz) packet shortcrust pastry
2 large onions, peeled and finely sliced
350 g (12 oz) bacon or chopped ham
1 tablespoon groundnut oil
1 kg (2 lbs) potatoes, peeled and thinly
   sliced – use a mandoline if available

1 tablespoon chopped herbs – I use thyme
   leaves
Generous rasping grated nutmeg
Milk and egg wash
175 ml (6 fl oz) double cream
Seasoning

Preheat the oven to 190°C/375°F/gas mark 5. Roll out the pastry and line a 20 cm (8 inch) springform tin. Keep enough to one side for a lid.

Fry the onions and bacon together in the groundnut oil until soft, then chop up the bacon into bits and transfer to a large bowl. Add the potatoes, herbs, seasoning and nutmeg and mix all together thoroughly. Turn into the pastry case and cover with the lid then glaze this with milk and egg wash. Cook for about 1¼ hours until the top is golden brown – if it colours too quickly then cover with some tinfoil. Remove from the heat and cut a hole in the top and push in a funnel then pour the cream through it. Replace the pastry circle and return to the oven to cook for a further 10 minutes.

Pissaladèrie

This is a Provençale-style pizza with a thin bread dough base. It's a cruise to make and toppings can, of course, be varied.

For the Base	Generous pinch of salt
225 g (8 oz) plain flour	3 tablespoons olive oil
1 egg	Warm water

Simply whiz these ingredients together in the food processor. It will be crumbly so trickle in a little warm water through the funnel until the dough forms a ball. Stop, remove from the bowl and wrap in cling-film. Leave to rest in the fridge for 30 minutes before rolling out on a floured surface then transfer to a rectangular ovenproof dish.

1 kg (2¼ lbs) onions, peeled and finely sliced	2 cloves garlic, peeled and finely chopped
1–2 tablespoons olive oil	1 tablespoon fresh thyme leaves
1 tablespoon soft brown sugar	6–8 anchovy fillets, drained and split in half lengthways
1 generous teaspoon Dijon mustard	2 tablespoons black olives
Pepper	

Preheat the oven to 190°C/375°F/gas mark 5. Prepare the filling by frying the onions very gently in the oil – add the sugar after about 10 minutes – and continue cooking until they are completely soft. Don't hurry this process, it does take time but remember, it can be done well in advance if more convenient. Blend in the mustard and some black pepper. Cover the dough with the onion mixture and top with the garlic and thyme leaves. Arrange the anchovies in a criss-cross pattern and dot around the olives then bake in the oven for 20–25 minutes until the edges have blistered brown and the pizza looks crisp and golden.

Tuna and Borlotti Bean Salad

1 large red onion, peeled and very finely
    sliced
1 tin of borlotti beans, drained and rinsed
Large handful flat leaf parsley leaves,
    coarsely chopped

1 tin of tuna in sunflower oil, drained of oil
    and roughly flaked
Squeeze of lemon juice
2–3 tablespoons olive oil

Arrange the ingredients in a flattish dish, mix together the oil and lemon juice, then season and pour over.

Feta, Pea and Cucumber Salad

100 g (4 oz) garden peas, podded
175 g (6 oz) Feta cheese – ewes' milk variety
    is best
Large cucumber

Small bunch mint leaves, roughly chopped
Seasoning
Vinaigrette

Peel, halve and seed the cucumber then chop into chunks and place in a colander and lightly salt. Cook the peas and when done, refresh immediately under cold water. Cube the feta and mix together in a bowl together with the cucumber and peas. Stir in the mint leaves, season generously with pepper (salt is not necessary) and lightly dress with the vinaigrette.

Tips from the Sink ～

- *To bulk this out more, add halved cherry tomatoes.*

- *Add some pea shoots if available.*

Dashers' Tapas

This is the savoury equivalent of the 'Pick 'n' Mix' sweetie counter. Though not designed to mirror a selection of authentic tapas, this makes perfect grazing food for sunny days. Make up a jug of Sangria and allow yourself to be transported, via Magic Carpet, to Spanish soil. In reality, however, this involves little more than a trip to the local deli. Just arrange everything in small dishes and bowls and stand these on two large platters so people can help themselves. Alternatively, add a large green salad and a basket of crusty bread and Salgamos a Comer!

Slices air-dried ham such as Iberico, Bayonne alongside a bowl of finest olive oil

Chunks of chorizo sausage

Roasted tomatoes with marjoram, lemon and cream

Aubergines with feta cheese and mint

Hummus or sour cream and chive dip

Buffalo mozzarella cheese torn up with avocado and basil

Potted shrimps

Selection of olives

Taramasalata – made from cods' roe – to avoid that blancmange pink gluck

Small squares of tortilla

Char-grilled artichoke hearts – available in jars

Elizabeth David's Piedmontese Peppers

I could go on and on but … I think you get the idea.

Lamb Kebabs with Crushed Minted Peas

Perfect garden fare when the barbecue is alight. Alternatively, cook these on top of the stove in a pan. Butterflied leg of lamb makes another option here to team up with the peas.

Wooden skewers, soaked in cold water for at least an hour

Leg or shoulder of lamb, trimmed up and cubed – allow 175 g (6 oz) meat per person

Olive oil

Seasoning

Sprigs rosemary

Thread the meat onto the skewers, anoint with a little olive oil and season well before cooking, either on the bbq, in a griddle pan on top of the stove or in a tray inside the oven, along with some rosemary sprigs. Turn several times during cooking until nicely done on all sides. This won't take long if the heat is up to speed – approximately 8–10 minutes.

For the Crushed Minted Peas

225 g (8 oz) petit pois

Pinch of sugar

Mint leaves, chopped

Dollop of crème fraîche

Clove of garlic, crushed

Few tablespoons of the cooking water from the peas

Seasoning

Cook the peas along with the sugar then drain and rinse under cold water, remembering to keep a little of the liquid to one side. Smash up in the processor together with the mint, crème fraîche, garlic and seasoning, running down the mixture to reach desired consistency. I make mine fairly loose so that it 'sauces' the meat. Arrange the kebabs on top of the purée and serve with buttery Jersey Royals.

Tip from the Sink ~

If no mint to hand, replace with mint sauce to taste.

Lemon Meringue Roulade

A faithful standby.

6 egg whites

275 g (10 oz) caster sugar

2 teaspoons cornflour

½ teaspoon white wine vinegar

1 jar lemon curd

Summer berries

Icing sugar

Preheat the oven to 180°C/350°F/gas mark 4. Beat the egg whites and gradually add the sugar. Fold in the cornflour and the vinegar and spoon into a large tray, lined with non-stick baking parchment. Cook for 30–35 minutes approximately and check to make sure the meringue is not taking on too much colour – if so, cover the top.

Remove from the heat, cover with a damp tea towel and, when cool, flip out onto a sheet of greaseproof paper sprinkled with icing sugar. Spread the surface with the lemon curd and some berries, then roll up lengthways and transfer to a flattish dish or basket and surround with the remaining fruits. Dust with icing sugar.

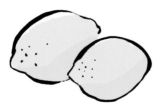

Chocolate Brownies

Compulsory picnic food – these taste as good as they smell. Err on the side of undercooking them for extra gooeyness.

225 g (8 oz) butter
75 g (3 oz) cocoa powder
100 g (4 oz) good quality plain chocolate – minimum 70% cocoa solids
4 eggs

½ teaspoon salt
450 g (1 lb) soft light brown sugar
100 g (4 oz) self-raising flour
175 g (6 oz) pecan nuts, lightly toasted and broken up

Preheat the oven to 180°C/350°F/gas mark 4. Lightly grease a roasting pan – mine is approximately 20 x 30 cm (8 x 12 inches). Melt the butter and stir in the cocoa powder then add the chocolate broken into squares. Stir until completely melted. Whisk eggs, salt and sugar until light and frothy then add the chocolate mixture. Next, fold in the flour and the nuts. Pour into the pan and cook for approximately 30 minutes so that they still feel slightly underdone. Cool in the tin before cutting up.

The Larder & the Cook's Equipment

The Larder

I have never actually lived in a house which boasted a larder though I've often dreamt of flinging open some door to reveal a cool outside walled room, stone flagged floor and shelves neatly stacked with all the comestibles a cook could require. In my fictitious world, this paragon of supreme orderliness would enable me to see, with one fleeting glance, every item. No rummaging around to look for that elusive jar of vanilla pods, the Pequillo peppers or the finest French mustard. All would be arranged neatly in serried rows, ingredient by ingredient and, most blissful of all, there would be no leaking or sticky-bottomed bottles or jars! The reality, however, is somewhat different although I must admit that I do try to keep my own kitchen cupboards reasonably tidy and everything does have its own place – more or less. This has less to do with an over-riding sense of compulsive organisation and more to do with the fact that I am invariably in a rush and resent wasting time in fruitless searches. Plus, if you had to open your cupboards upon occasion to a clutch of people who have come to a demo, then you would want all inside to be *comme il faut* – 'just so'. Just like the knicker drawer, really – if not colour-coded!

The list of 'essentials' here is merely a reflection of what I like to have to hand. To some, it may appear woefully inadequate or non-cheffy – more Aga than Prada – whereas others may feel I have sufficient scope and stock to hand to open up my own specialist food shop – Harvey Nichols Fifth Floor move over! Your particular style of cooking will dictate how and with what you fill your own store space and, like any sort of shopping, this is down to individual taste. I tend to replace items as I use them rather than waiting until I actually need them the next time – only to discover they are not there. This way, shopping for a hastily arranged supper party is far less onerous. A regular trawl through the shelves pays dividends since it will remind you to throw out and replace aged dried herbs, packets of prunes and exotic rices and pulses which are well past their sell-by date. For this reason alone, I only ever buy small bags of ingredients such as flour to avoid opening them up and then leaving them for longer than one should before using again.

Oils – these include sunflower, groundnut, vegetable plus several different types and grades of olive oil from a light one for everyday cooking uses through to the real McCoy used as a lubricant for ciabatta bread and salads, plus different flavoured nut oils and some truffle oil. And when I think about it, I sometimes make my own herby oil infusions.

Vinegars – balsamic. There is no such thing as good, 'cheap' balsamic. Choose only that which has been aged in wooden casks. It will be dark in colour and makes, I always think, a popular present for a foodie friend. Also, sherry, cider, tarragon, Cabernet Sauvignon red wine, ordinary white wine, shallot, rice and fruit vinegars, such as raspberry.

Sea salt – either Maldon or a French variety such as Gros Sel. Whole black peppercorns and whole white peppercorns and in two separate grinders. I have no truck with those jars of multi-coloured peppercorns.

Mustards – wholegrain, French Dijon and Maille, tarragon mustard, English

Bars of plain, dark chocolate – 70% cocoa solids, and good quality white chocolate.

Packets of nuts – hazel, pecan, pine, macadamia.

Bottled Passata sauce, tinned tomatoes, tomato purée and sun-dried tomato paste.

Tinned anchovies, tuna, consommé soup, Heinz tomato soup, beans – flageolet, cannelloni, borlotti, chick peas, sweetcorn.

Spices and herbs: juniper berries, saffron, coriander seeds, Chinese five spice powder, curry powder, star anise – both whole and ground, cardamon seeds, cloves and ground cloves, celery salt, chilli flakes, cumin, paprika, cayenne, whole nutmegs, cinnamon – both powder and sticks … and so on.

Vanilla pods.

Leaf gelatine.

Jars Pequillo peppers, sun-dried tomatoes, marinated artichokes, capers, olives, goose fat, cornichons, gerkins and capers.

Sauces: soy sauces – light and dark, hoisin sauce, fish sauce – Nam Pla, teriyaki sauce, oyster sauce.

Coconut milk.

Condensed milk.

Chestnut puree.

Dried mushrooms including morel, porcini.

Chicken stock cubes.

Treacle, honey, maple and golden syrup.

Sugars: granulated and caster, unrefined, soft brown, molasses, palm sugar, icing sugar, La Perrouche sugar lumps (when I am feeling extravagant!).

Saffron.

Rice and pasta: risotto – Caranoli, wild rice, spaghetti, paparadelle and taglietelle, glass and oriental noodles.

Cous-cous and lentils.

Flour: plain and self-raising, wholemeal and potato flour.

Cream of tartar, bicarbonate of soda, baking powder.

Orange and rose-flavoured flower waters.

Vanilla essence.

Cook's Equipment

When I hear the phrase *batterie de cuisine* being bandied around it always make me giggle conjuring up, as it does, visions of great truckloads of every conceivable type of culinary gadget. My own collection of pots and pans is a modest assortment, though experience has taught me that it is better to invest in a few good quality, heavy-based, saucepans which conduct the heat properly and cook evenly rather than a large selection of light-weight alternatives which soon prove inferior. My chopping boards are hardly in their first flush of youth and whereas I do have a modern melamine one, I still use my lovely old wooden ones, and to hell with Health and Safety. Sometimes, Health and Safety rules push themselves too far! The danger, of course, in buying endless machines for this and machines for that often boils down to a question of storage (let alone expense). Deep-fat fryers, bread-making machines, fish kettles, juicers, sets of copper pans, cumbersome meat slicers and coffee machines are all very well but demand that precious commodity – space. Plus they are usually cumbersome yet, at the same time, fiddly to wash up. More often than not, they are consigned to the tops of cupboards never to be fetched down – only to gather a thick layer of dust. I will admit, though, I am fond of my ice-cream maker and I could not live without the dishwasher which trundles away continuously. Once again, though, it is all about what works for you as to which particular items you feel you cannot live without. And I most certainly could not survive without my knives and guard these preciously. Each one has its own job and all are peculiarly personal to me. They are all, also, extremely sharp which saves one a lot of time and effort. My friendly butcher sees to this for me.

2 griddle ridged heavy cast iron pans – one for fish, another for meat and vegetables

Omelette pan

Non-stick frying pans and a cast iron frying pan

Saucepans with lids – heavy non-stick

Mouli-legumes for mashed potato

Large pan with detachable handle for oven use

Mixing bowls in varying sizes

Pestle and mortar

Several chopping boards

Metal skewers and tongs

Oven thermometer

Nutmeg grater

Kitchen scissors

Swivel peeler

Cooking spoons – wooden, slatted and metal

Wire whisks – in several sizes

Mircoplane graters

Icing sugar shaker

Sauce bottles for squirting

Magimix

Ice-cream maker

Coffee grinder especially for herbs

Hand-held electric stick

Electric hand whisk

Fine mesh sieves in varying sizes

Cake rack

Wooden rolling pin

Index

anchovy butter 140
asparagus, griddled with curried mayonnaise 41
aubergine, spinach and tomato, tian of 162
avocado soup with prawns 34

beef, fillet of 109
beef, Thai salad 61
beetroot, jellied with prawns 38
beetroot, oven roasted 164
borscht and cranberry soup 32
bloody Mary 161
blue cheese and pear salad, roasted 65
bread sauce 141
bullshot 37
butternut and carrot puree 168
butternut and pinenut salad, roasted 66

Caraffini sauce 146
casseroled lamb 108
cauliflower cheese cottage pie 110
celeriac and celery soup 28
celeriac and Jerusalem artichoke mousse 45
celeriac remoulade 56
cheese sables 152
cheesey wafers 158
cherries with white chocolate sauce 128
chicken escalopes, griddled lemon and herb 85
chicken liver parfait 40
chicken thighs with herbs and sea salt 175
chicken *see also* Thai chick
chocolate brownies 182
chocolate cake (soft) 125
chocolate fondant puddings (hot) 119
chocolate ice cream 134

chocolate sauce 147
crab and broad bean bruschetta 52
crab tart 52
crème brulee with plums 135
crèpes Suzette (cheat's) 121
cucumber and mint soup 174
cucumber, pickled 163
curried parsnip and apple soup 36

domestic god's salad 62
drinks 159–61
duck, oriental 98
duck with glazed turnips and honey 101
duck with hedgerow sauce 100
duck legs, sweet and sour 99

Easter egg salad 70
eggy bread 153
elderflower cordial 160
elderflower jelly 129
Eton mess 126

feta, pea and cucumber salad 178
fig and walnut tart 122
fish, baked with herbs 74
fish in salt crust 75
fishcakes 76
fish pie, Monte Carlo 80
fish, steamed fillets of 77
flapjacks 157
flat leaf parsley and shallot salad
French onion soup 30
fudgey fruit 118

game terrine 46
gazpacho soup 33
ginger biscuit pudding 136
ginger semi-freddo 133
Gougere puffs 152
green beans with hazelnuts 55
grouse, roast with red wine gravy 93

Hollandaise sauce 144

ice bowl 130
iced delights, instant 131

Jerusalem artichoke and cannellini bean soup 29

kitchen suppers 71–112
   fish 72–83
   game 92–101
   meat 102–11
   poultry 84–91
lamb, herb crusted rack of 105
lamb, Jonathan's 107
lamb kebabs 180
lamb, loin of 106
larder and cook's equipment 183–8
lemon curd 150
lemon drink 159
lemon drizzle cake 156
lemon meringue roulade 181

mayonnaise 143
meringues Mont Blanc 124
mushroom mousses (warm) 44
mussels, tagliatelle of 83

omelette terrine 173
orange Easter biscuits
orange see also Seville orange

parsley potager 27
partridge, roast with leek, orange and

cardamon sauce 94
pear, Parma ham and goat's cheese salad 59
pesto sauce 146
petit pois 163
pheasant breasts 96
pheasant in orange with gin 95
picnics 172–82
pigeon salad (warm) 80
pigeon with pomegranate dressing 97
pineapple (roasted) and kirsch pudding 120
pissaladèrie 177
pork, roast belly of 103
pork tenderloin 104
potatoes 165–7, 176
potato pie 176
potato, rocket and fresh truffles 165
potatoes, baked with snails 166
potatoes, sautéed in goose fat 167
poulet de Licques and Farci 86
prawn, melon and cucumber cocktail 51
puddings 113–36

quail, stuffed 90
quail with tomato and tarragon vinaigrette 91

raspberry sauce 148
rhubarb, ginger and orange crumble 115

salade Nicoise 68
salads 57–70, 178
salmon with Pernod sauce 81
salmon with pesto and Parma ham 175
salmon with red cabbage 78
salsa verde 149
sauce Bordelaise 145
Sauce Poivrade 148
sauces, standbys and sides 137–68
   sauces 140–9
   sides 162–4
   standbys 150–7
savouries 158

Index

scallops, grilled and bacon salad 64
scallops, seared with Jerusalem artichoke
    purée 82
Seville orange marmalade 151
Seville orange sponge 117
shellfish bisque 34
smoked haddock and saffron soup 31
smoked haddock, ceviche of 54
smoked mackerel pâté 174
soda bread 155
soups 27–37, 174
spinach soufflé with anchovy sauce 42
Sportsman's Special 154
starters 38–56
sticky toffee pudding 116

Stilton and strawberry jam toasts 158
strawberry tart 132
strawberries in lime syrup 127
summer's day salad 66

tapas 179
Thai chick, Fred's 88
tomato and basil galette 50
tomato pudding 48
tortilla 172
tuna and borlotti bean salad

veal, roast loin of 112
vinaigrette 142